The Mountains of Rasselas

THOMAS PAKENHAM

Text and Photographs by Thomas Pakenham

The Mountains of Rasselas

An Ethiopian Adventure by

THOMAS PAKENHAM

Contents

For V.
and in memory of Ann Roberts

Foreword

This January, 1998, I hired a helicopter from an American missionary in Addis Ababa and made one last attempt to land on a mountain in Ethiopia that had haunted my dreams for nearly half a century.

The mountain is called Wehni, meaning prison in Amharic, and it became a kind of royal 'larder'. For 200 years successive Emperors put their sons into cold storage on its summit to keep them out of mischief. The custom captured the imagination of Europe, and inspired Dr Johnson's improving tale, *Rasselas, Prince of Abissinia.*

The postscript to this new edition describes the latest twist in my protracted love-affair with the Mountain.

Forty-two years earlier, I had set off across the high plateau on a three-day journey by mule to discover where the Mountain was and whether I could climb it. I was 22, raw from Oxford, and (why conceal it now?) on the rebound from unrequited love. Beside me rode the local governor, revolver in his Sam Browne belt, with half a dozen wild-looking retainers carrying rusty rifles running beside us.

In a modest way I fancied myself as an explorer, in the steps of James Bruce, the enterprising Scottish laird who came to the Ethiopian capital, Gondar, in 1770. No European, I was assured, had hitherto set eyes on the Mountain, let alone climbed it – although Bruce left a hearsay account of Wehni and the fate of the princes on the summit.

Bruce adopted oriental dress on his travels. For the ascent of the Mountain, I myself wore the flowing white jitterbub of an Ethiopian country gentleman. Perhaps I was emotionally retarded, an innocent, certainly a romantic.

Does it all sound more than a little absurd? But half a century ago Ethiopia, too, was retarded, somewhat innocent, and undeniably romantic.

In the capital, Addis Ababa, peasants would prostrate themselves on the pavement before Haile Selassie, as the cavalcade of Rolls-Royces swept down the potholed streets. The Lion of Judah had already ruled longer than most people could remember (he had proclaimed himself Regent in 1916) and in 1955 seemed more like a god than an Emperor.

Out in the country life continued much as it had in the days of Bruce – or indeed in the medieval world of Prester John encountered by the Portuguese embassy, the first Europeans to reach Ethiopia and be allowed to return home.

When you stayed in the house o[...] the open hearth and smoke blac[...] roof above your head. Oxen wer[...] protect them from wild beasts. P[...] white-cloaked during the week, [...] brocade on Sundays. The Churc[...]

Between attempts to conqu[...] recesses of the high plateau east [...] Europeans had ever travelled, an[...] unrecorded medieval church called Bethlehem. My discovery rated four pages in the *Illustrated London News*. This was the golden age for the amateur in Ethiopia.

After I left Ethiopia in 1956, an Australian explorer landed on the summit in a helicopter. Then a team of British army cadets climbed Wehni and pronounced it, a sheer rock 1,000 feet high, even more formidable than I had claimed.

As for the medieval church at Bethlehem, other exciting discoveries were made by my successors: unrecorded rock churches and cave churches. But I am told that nothing can hold a candle, architecturally speaking, to the church at Bethlehem. I even received a kindly accolade from His Imperial Majesty.

What amazes me now is that the patriarch I encountered in 1956 enjoyed nineteen more years of imperial power. Then in his eighty-third year came the deluge, and the old Ethiopia we knew vanished downstream.

The Emperor was murdered in secret by the Derg (Shadow) led by Colonel Menghistu. Most of the great feudal magnates who had governed Ethiopia under the Emperor were also swept away in the revolution. Sadly, I must record the death of Ras Asserate Kassa, my generous host. He was shot, with fifty-nine other leading lights of the old regime, in the cellars of the palace in November 1974. Without Asserate Kassa I would have achieved nothing. I salute his memory – and that of other kindly patrons who guided my steps across the green fastnesses of Ethiopia in my impatient youth.

In preparing this new edition I have added various photographs, including twenty in colour taken this year. I have also corrected a few misjudgements in spelling (there is no agreed way to transcribe many Amharic names) and excised some of the detail that seemed irrelevant to the main narrative. Otherwise I have left the book as I wrote it: a

FOREWORD

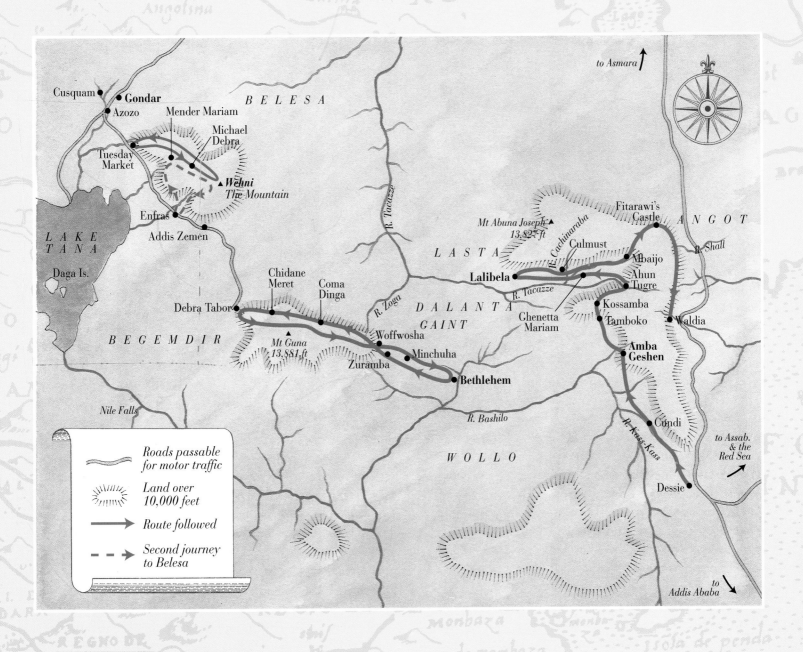

ABOVE: *The route map showing my mule journeys to the Mountain, to Bethlehem, and to Amba Geshen and Lalibela. Debra Damo, which I visited by car, is in Tigre, north of this map.*

OVERLEAF, PAGE 9: *The text in the centre of this map reads: 'In Amara Monte Aethiopii imperatoris filii et nepotes in custodiis ... detinentur ... et vacatis imperiis successor educitur' ('On Mount Amara the sons and nephews of the Ethiopian emperor are kept in prison ... and from there, when the throne is vacant, the successor is brought down.'). Aethiopia (Abyssinia), Johan Blaeu, c. 1635, Royal Geographical Society.*

period piece. 'He sighs like Orsino,' complained one reviewer. Yes, I was very young.

For this new edition I remain in the debt of George Weidenfeld and his firm which published the original version. I owe special thanks to Anthony Cheetham, Michael Dover, Penny Gardiner and Nick Clark, and also to my agent, Mike Shaw. Friends who have given me invaluable help for this edition include: Robby Roberts, David Buxton, Amaha Kassa, Asfa Wossen Asserate, Michael Imru, Robin and Merril Christopher, Gordon and Rosemary Wetherall, Richard Illingworth, Richard and Rita Pankhurst, Jane Taylor, John Johnson, Mark Girouard and Kenneth Rose.

Finally, I should like to thank two of my children, Eliza and Fred, and my son-in-law, Alex, who accompanied me to Ethiopia this year, and touched hands, across the void of centuries, with the empire of Prester John.

Acknowledgements are gratefully given to Susan Benson (Campbell) for the line drawings which appear throughout the book, which illustrated the 1959 edition.

Prologue

> According to the custom which has descended from age to age among the monarchs of the torrid zone, Rasselas was confined in a private palace, with the other sons and daughters of Abyssinian royalty, till the order of succession should call him to the throne.
>
> Dr Johnson: *Rasselas*

In May 1955 I had been dining in a Venetian Gothic house overlooking the Thames at Oxford. We had begun to talk of amusing places where we might spend the summer holidays after Schools. Abyssinia cropped up frequently in the conversation. The place had exciting associations for us all – was this not the land of Prester John and the Queen of Sheba, the birthplace of Evelyn Waugh's *Black Mischief* and *Scoop*? After Tibet, Abyssinia sounded the most exotic place for a holiday. None of us, however, had the money to finance so long a journey, and the idea languished. A friend and I decided to spend the summer wandering around the Levant.

Here matters would have rested had I not happened to mention the scheme to a Dominican priest who was a well-known authority on Byzantium and the Eastern Church. As a Byzantinist he had travelled to many of the remotest parts of the world, and he knew all about Abyssinia, alias Ethiopia, the modern name for the country. 'Listen, Thos,' he said. 'Have you ever thought of doing any serious explorations? When I was travelling some years ago...' My eyes strayed from the black clerical clothes to the dog-collar held together with paper-clips; it was odd to think of this gentle academic figure disputing with the fanatic priests of the Orient, bargaining with bloodthirsty Tuaregs over some Byzantine sherd. 'I was travelling in Ethiopia and I was very tempted to go to the Mountain near Gondar called "Wachni". The Kings' sons were confined there ... Johnson describes the customs in *Rasselas* ... you'll find its actual history in Bruce's *Travels* ... Here, I'll write you a note to the nephew of the Governor-General.'

A few days later I rang up the Byzantinist in the vague hope of some practical details. But he had already flown out on a quest for Athenian pottery in the jungles of Malaya; he would be incommunicado there for several months.

Then one day an air-letter arrived from Malaya. Inside were half a dozen lines of spidery writing crawling across the page somewhat after the manner of a surrealist poem: 'My dear Thos,' it read. 'Delighted that you're going to Ethiopia. I won't fuss you with any more boring details about Wachni now. My last word of advice is don't underplay your relationship with Lord Valentia: the Ethiopian notion of stock is a very exacting one. When you come back I shall arrange for the *Illustrated London News* to print something about your discoveries ...' The letter ran on for a few lines more about a few excitements of the country I shouldn't miss – the pagan obelisks of Axum, the tenth-century church of Debra Damo, the ruined cathedral built by Spanish Jesuits – then ended with a repeated injunction to act the aristocrat. About the Mountain he had added nothing.

However, he at least gave me the sources for the history of this lost Mountain. In the leisurely weeks after Schools I read up all that was known about Gondar and Wachni.

One of the most melodramatic features of the highlands of Ethiopia was apparently the wealth of mountains called 'ambas'. Travellers described them as flat-topped, sheer-sided mountains – fingers and thumbs of rock that broke the flat horizons of the tableland with their extravagant silhouettes. Three of these ambas played a crucial role in Ethiopian history. Indeed together they straddled a thousand years of this history and linked two shadowy worlds, the medieval Christian empire of Prester John with the pre-Christian Axumite world of the Queen of Sheba.

Sheba, alias Saba, land of the Sabeans, was the corner of South Arabia from where the biblical Queen of Sheba had set off to visit King Solomon of Israel. The story is told in both 1 Kings and 2 Chronicles in the Old Testament. In real life the Sabeans were one of the powerful Semitic tribes who formed an overseas colony – theirs a kind of new Sheba – on the west side of the Red Sea. Here, in a green tableland intersected with canyons, similar in scenery and climate to their homeland, they settled in what is today northern Ethiopia and Eritrea.

The new settlers traded and raided for slaves, gold and ivory. Genetically they were soon merged with Africans of Cushitic stock with whom they intermarried. But culturally

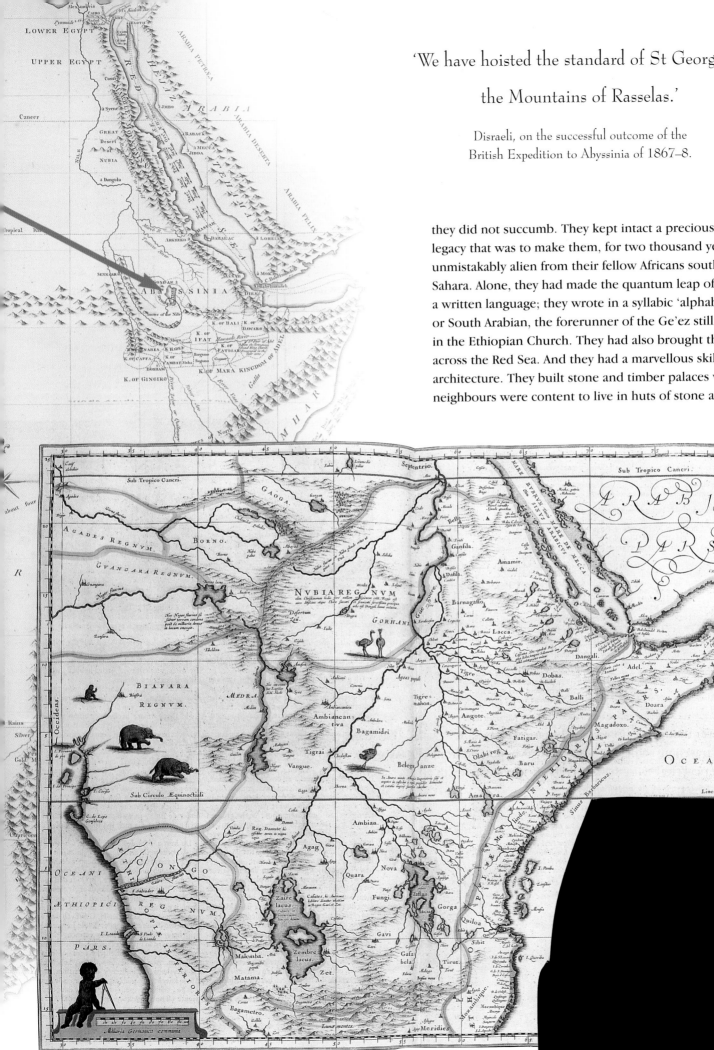

'We have hoisted the standard of St George on the Mountains of Rasselas.'

Disraeli, on the successful outcome of the British Expedition to Abyssinia of 1867–8.

they did not succumb. They kept intact a precious Semitic legacy that was to make them, for two thousand years, unmistakably alien from their fellow Africans south of the Sahara. Alone, they had made the quantum leap of developing a written language; they wrote in a syllabic 'alphabet', Sabean or South Arabian, the forerunner of the Ge'ez still used today in the Ethiopian Church. They had also brought the plough across the Red Sea. And they had a marvellous skill in architecture. They built stone and timber palaces where their neighbours were content to live in huts of stone and mud.

In due course the city–state of Axum, at the south-west of the tableland, absorbed its neighbours. The Axumites became masters of both sides of the Red Sea, subjugating even Sheba and the peoples like the Habashat from whom they were descended (and from whom Abyssinia took its name). At Axum, in the precincts of the temples dedicated to the South Arabian gods of the sun and the moon, rose sixty or seventy extraordinary obelisks. These included the tallest monolithic stone ever erected in the ancient world. Still more astonishing than their height was their character. In Egypt the obelisks were decorated with hieroglyphs to please the gods. At Axum they were representations of half-timbered

First clue to the quest proposed to me by the Byzantinist – pagan relics of the Queen of Sheba at Axum. The Ethiopian empire once stretched from the Nile to South Arabia.

FAR LEFT AND CENTRE: *The tallest standing obelisk at Axum carved out of granite to represent a nine-storey palace.*

LEFT: *A thousand years later the Axumite style was still alive and well in the Christian rock churches of Lalibela.*

skyscrapers, surmounted with emblems of the sun and the moon. In height they were the same as the originals, 60 to 100 feet high, with full-scale wooden doors and windows accurately carved out of granite. Only in width and breadth were they reduced to the scale of models.

So this was the African Sheba, the terror of its neighbours on both sides of the Red Sea, whose monarch was certainly the leading African monarch known to the Graeco-Roman world two centuries after the birth of Christ.

In AD 313 Constantine recommended Christianity to all the subjects of the Roman empire. Three decades later Ezana, King of Axum, anxious to enlist the help of the Byzantine navy against Persian invaders, followed his lead. Missionaries from Syria and authorities of what became the Coptic church of Egypt were glad to provide assistance. Ethiopia's first Christian bishop was a Syrian slave turned evangelist, con-secrated by the Coptic patriarch at Alexandria. The link with Coptic Egypt was forged by the great controversy about the nature of Christ that tore the Christian world apart in 451. Ethiopia followed Egypt into the monophysite camp, and for more than 1,000 years the head of the Ethiopian church, the Abuna, was always an Egyptian monk from Alexandria.

Meanwhile, as the Axumites extended eastwards into their old Sabean homelands, Jewish emigrants from Palestine had been pushing south, conquering, colonizing and converting pagan South Arabia. We can only guess at the impact on Axum of these rival imperialists. In the Ethiopian version of the biblical story, the Queen of Sheba, alias Queen Makeda, leaves Axum to pay her respects to King Solomon in Israel. She sleeps with the king (he tricks her into surrender) and returns to Axum pregnant with a son, who becomes Menelik I, the founder of the so-called 'Solomonic' line of emperors, culminating in the present Emperor, Haile Selassie. What is certain is that, before Christianity was brought to Ethiopia, a primitive form of Judaism had spread there from South Arabia. A small minority of Ethiopians remained 'Jewish'; these were to become the Falashas or 'black Jews' of today. Most Axumites became Christian, but their Christianity took an unusually Judaized form. They kept the Jewish Sabbath, added to the Christian Sabbath; they kept the Jewish taboos about unclean meat and unclean women; the most sacred object in every Ethiopian church was (and is) the Ark of the Covenant, representing the original which Ethiopians claimed had been stolen from Solomon and brought to Axum by Menelik I.

Still more potent for the future was a political idea that had travelled south with the Jews: the King of Ethiopia and his people were the heirs to Solomon and the children of Israel, the elect of God. Axum, the new Sheba, had become the new Jerusalem.

Second clue to my instructions from the Byzantinist: relics of the Christian empire of Prester John. LEFT TO RIGHT: *The Cathedral of Mary at Axum (photographed by me and fresco); a processional cross from Amba Geshen, the second prison-mountain; and the tenth-century church of Debra Damo, on the first prison-mountain.*

Meanwhile Axum had reached its apogee with the coming of Christianity and then sunk into slow decline. By the end of the seventh century Persian fleets in the Red Sea, followed by the relentless surge of Islam, had extinguished Axum's empire overseas. Soon the country and its people had vanished behind a curtain of increasingly hostile Moslem powers. In Gibbon's famous words: 'the Aethiopians slept near a thousand years, forgetful of the world, by whom they were forgotten.' (*Decline and Fall*, XLVII) In fact Ethiopian chronicles record that it was during this shadowy millennium that the first two of the prison-mountains – Debra Damo and Amba Geshen – played their crucial part in Ethiopian history.

The monastery on the summit of Debra Damo, in the northern province of Tigre, had been founded by one of the 'Nine Saints' – missionaries from Syria in the fifth century. By the ninth century it was the oldest church in the country, except for the Cathedral of Mary at Axum, and a famous centre of learning. Flat-topped and sheer-sided, the amba was also a natural fortress, believed impregnable to attack.

Hence its choice as a prison for the princes of the Solomonic line when the Emperor decided to put them on an amba in order to keep them out of mischief.

How long it served this grim purpose the chronicles do not reveal; perhaps for a century or more. Then in the ninth century the Solomonic throne was seized by a mysterious usurping queen called Yudit (Judith), variously described as a pagan or a Jew. Somehow Queen Yudit captured Debra Damo, stripped the church of its treasures and put to the sword all the princes imprisoned there.

The Zagre dynasty from Lasta who followed Queen Yudit was soon tamed. Prudently they turned Christian, and in due course decided that their own princes of the blood would be safer put away on a mountain top. Hence the choice of Amba Geshen close to Lasta. Like Debra Damo, it was flat-topped and supposed impregnable. A church was founded there early in the Middle Ages. For a century or so it became the royal storehouse for the safekeeping of the Zagre royal family. Then, after 1270 when the Solomonic dynasty was somehow restored by Yekun Imlac, Amba Geshen (also known as Amba Israel because of the princes' pedigree) continued as a royal prison for the next three centuries.

It is at the end of this period, in the 1520s, that we have our first glimpse of the mountain and the princes seen through European eyes.

By now the Ethiopians' 1,000-year long sleep was over, and the Emperor was fully awake and desperately signalling to Christian Europe to save him from his Moslem enemies. In 1517 the Ottoman Sultan sent a Turkish fleet to seize the port of Massawah and seal off Ethiopia's main outlet to the Red Sea. At the same time a storm-cloud of local Moslems – Somalis and Hararis from the eastern lowlands – was poised ready to burst over the Christian tableland.

The SOS to Europe was answered. But by then it was almost too late.

Already, at the end of the fifteenth century, the tale was current in Europe that a powerful Christian monarch, called Prester John, ruled somewhere in the wilds of Africa. Reports from Ethiopian monks in Jerusalem, and a royal envoy from Africa, seemed to confirm the identification of Prester John with the Emperor of Ethiopia. In 1520 an embassy was sent there by the King of Portugal, whose fleets had recently founded an empire in Goa and the Indies. The chaplain to the embassy, Francisco Alvarez, returned to Europe and published the first fully documented, eye-witness account of Ethiopia and its exotic brand of Christianity. This included the strange story of the sons of Prester John imprisoned on the summit of Amba Geshen.

The Portuguese embassy had left in 1526, privileged to witness the last moments of glory, so to speak, of Prester John. Next year the Moslem storm-cloud burst over the Christian tableland. Imam Ahmed, known as Gran (the Left-handed) began an annual series of campaigns to burn and loot every church in the country, killing and enslaving the population. The Emperor took refuge where he could – in caves, in bogs, on mountain-tops, including Debra Damo. Turkish musketeers sent from Massawah added their muscle to the invasion.

Even Amba Geshen, believed impregnable, was captured by the Imam's troops after a vengeful Ethiopian had betrayed a secret path to the summit. The nation's treasury was taken, the princes of the blood massacred.

Meanwhile the King of Portugal, reassured by the reports of Alvarez and the others that Prester John was alive and well and living in Ethiopia, decided to send a party of 400 musketeers led by Christopher da Gama. He was the son of the Vasco da Gama who had pioneered the sea-route to the Indies. But his small military mission arrived in Ethiopia only to find the Christian empire dissolving before their eyes.

Fortunately for the Emperor, a long run of easy victories had gulled Gran into over-confidence. In 1541 he was shot by one of Da Gama's musketeers at the Battle of Wainedega near Lake Tana. The victory proved decisive. And for nearly a century successive Emperors showed their faith in Europe by encouraging Catholic missionaries from Portugal and Spain.

The most successful was a Spanish Jesuit, Fr. Paez, who built a cathedral at Gorgora for the Emperor Suseneyos.

In the 1620s, however, the Emperor Suseneyos went too far – so it appeared to the majority of his Christian subjects. He announced his conversion to Catholicism. His successor Facilidas reversed the policy, expelling the Catholic missionaries or martyring those who stayed. With the help of Indian masons he built a capital at Gondar. He then re-instituted the custom of his ancestors: the Emperor's sons were locked away on an amba. Wehni, fifty miles from Gondar, was the amba now chosen for a prison.

The picturesque custom of imprisoning the King's relations captured the imagination of Europe. It forms the basis for Johnson's moral tale of Rasselas, the Prince of Abyssinia who was confined in a Happy Valley overhung with high mountains precluding his escape.

The principal sources for Rasselas were accounts of Amba Geshen. But at the time Johnson wrote Rasselas, Amba Geshen had been replaced by Wehni. Probably Johnson knew nothing about this third amba. It was not until twenty years after Rasselas was published that James Bruce of Kinnaird returned to England to give a full description of the Court of the Abyssinian King at Gondar where he had spent two years, and to retail many exotic stories about the nearby Mountain (Bruce calls it Wechne) where the King himself had been confined prior to his succession. Dr Johnson, whose Rasselas owed so much to the dark institution of the Mountain, joined with Horace Walpole in a bitter attack on

Bruce, calling him the Abyssinian liar – a reference to his engraving of the Abyssinian lyre or dulcimer. The eventual publication of Bruce's book, *Travels to Discover the Source of the Nile*, merely added fuel to the controversy.

Now Bruce did not pretend to have visited this third amba in person. As it was still in use the approaches were closely guarded, and Bruce never got within thirty miles of it; he marked the road to the Mountain petering out into the mountains of Belesa. After the Mountain was abandoned, European travellers might have been expected to visit the place. But none apparently had had the chance (or the inclination) to seek it out and put an end to all speculation on the predicament of the princes who were imprisoned there. The earlier prison-mountains had been visited at various times since the Portuguese entered the country. The third Mountain of Rasselas apparently remained, I concluded from diligent research in the reading-room of the British Museum, unvisited by any European.

I had now unravelled the words of the Byzantinist. He was suggesting that I should be the first to give the world an eye-witness account of the Mountain. If successful the quest would add something – though exactly what was obscure at this moment – to our historical knowledge of a vexed period in Ethiopian history. I might also have the satisfaction of vindicating Bruce. And the quest would be spiced by the romantic associations of Rasselas.

The practical difficulties, it appeared, of finding the actual site of the Mountain were not to be dismissed lightly. As no European had apparently visited the place, it was not to be expected that the maps of the area would be of any use. This surmise was confirmed by a visit to the map-room of the British Museum. The maps of Abyssinia seemed very sketchy and many areas close to Gondar itself were marked as unexplored; of the Mountain there was no sign. I should

have to rely on the vague directions in Bruce's *Travels*, supplemented by inquiries about the Mountain when I reached Gondar. But inquiries were not going to be easy. I was not even certain of the Mountain's correct name: the Byzantinist's version was 'Wachni', Bruce's 'Wechne', the Royal Chronicles of Abyssinia recorded 'Wahni' – all forms of the Amharic word 'Wehni' meaning 'prison'. I had an uneasy suspicion that if I ever reached Gondar I should find an embarrassingly large number of mountains to choose from.

Despite this difficulty, and the equally formidable obstacle to the expedition in the shape of the cost, the idea was definitely intriguing. All that I had read about Ethiopia confirmed my original impression that it would be an exciting place in which to travel. Outside the capital and the scattered towns on the infrequent motor-roads, life apparently still went on today as it had in the days of Bruce. In the deep country the extraordinary Ethiopian Orthodox Church, which numbered Herod and Alexander the Great among its saints, and claimed to have the Ark of the Covenant locked within the holy city of Axum, was still most powerful. I would be in close contact with the strange priests of this Church. I might also be able to see something of their unique medieval architecture. Of the difficulties in travelling in the deep country I knew little, though I read with alarm the reports of bandits that all books on Ethiopia contain.

Eventually, more with an eye to impress my friends than with any serious hope or intention of making the journey, I put out the news that I was off to Ethiopia. The reaction of my friends was most warm-hearted. I found myself regarded with the special awe granted to the explorer. One gave me a bundle of cleft sticks to enable me to send her word of the progress of the expedition; another leaked the news to the social columnist of a Sunday paper. He rang me up. I made a brief and dignified statement announcing my intentions, and read next week 'that with kit-bag and water-bottle [I was] going to discover the lost city of Gondar'.

I had in fact a suitcase, and possessed no water-bottle, while Gondar is still today a city of some fifty thousand people. But I could not complain about the publicity I had received; the Features Editor of a London daily newspaper read the piece and suggested I should try to write some travel articles for them. These might go some way to paying the expense of the journey to Ethiopia. Yet I was still far from clear in my own mind whether I would go there even if I could. Postponing all such decisions, I set off for the Near East, fleeing before the results of Schools, like those American householders who are said to leap into their motor-cars and drive madly away before the path of an approaching hurricane.

I was in Aden in late October. I had heard from some journalists I had met that in early November the twenty-fifth anniversary of the Emperor's Jubilee would be celebrated in Addis Ababa. It would be an excellent moment to arrive; I should be able to see something of the country as a tourist before I began my journey to the Mountain.

To the early travellers and traders, the deserts between

BELOW LEFT: AN *Amhara woman with hair plaited and buttered.*
BELOW RIGHT: *Spinning cotton, as it has been spun for two millennia,
at the door of a hut.*
TOP: *Danakil women, painted by J. Bernatz in 1841, and*
BELOW CENTRE, *one photographed by me in 1956.*
RIGHT: *Perhaps I was rather over-dressed myself.*

the Ethiopian highlands and the Red Sea were a formidable obstacle. Arthur Rimbaud, with a caravan of guns for King Menelik, took over four months to cross this wasteland. For me, looking down from an aeroplane 14,000 feet up, the desert seemed as innocent as the sandy floor of a rock pool.

At first sight the country looked familiarly European: even the irregular clusters of African huts appeared from this height like mushrooms languidly scattered from an aeroplane. But the illusion of familiarity soon left one. A pink canyon cut across our path, separating by a gap of half a mile or so two identical slices of plateau, and in the black depths of the canyon a river gleamed for a moment in the sun, crawling painfully towards a rendezvous with the Blue Nile a hundred miles to the west. This was at once unfamiliar and exciting. The tremendous erosion of the rains washing against the plateau had carved out that canyon. It must have been several thousand feet lower at its bed than the surrounding tableland.

Minutes later the landscape changed again, as the ground began to fall away to the south; we had reached the southern rim of the plateau. The villages became larger and more richly endowed with groves of gum trees. We were nearing Addis Ababa.

Soon the tree-tops rose up to greet us in their thousands. The bottle-green of the mature eucalyptus, the caper-blue of the young saplings, hid the gleaming roofs of Addis Ababa in a blue-green mist. The plane banked and landed.

We stepped out, and were welcomed by a gust of sharp mountain air, and a fragrant aroma of eucalyptus leaves.

We stepped out, and were welcomed by a gust of sharp mountain air, and a fragrant aroma of eucalyptus leaves.

1
Chapter One

Twenty-five years later, after a ruthless invasion and occupation by the Fascist forces of Mussolini, Addis Ababa, under the aegis of the Emperor is a large city with a population approaching half a million, with mile after mile of paved streets, with radio stations ... airfields ... a golf club ... a stadium ... a horse-racing tract and many similar amenities.

From the official hand-out describing the Coronation Jubilee

The Emperor's Jubilee

Addis Ababa, the new flower of Menelik's empire, the window through which Ethiopia looks out on the world and the world looks in on Ethiopia. At first sight it seemed as bizarre a place as any tourist could wish for. As I drove to the hotel recommended to me the taxi hooted continuously, turning a brown furrow of passers-by; the sun threw crisp, indigo shadows across the metalled roads. I felt exultant and light-headed. The altitude was like a glass of sherry on an empty stomach.

Addis Ababa is both a town and a village. High up on the slopes of Entotto, over 9,000 feet above sea-level, the northern outposts of Addis grapple with the uniformly green ranks of eucalyptus trees. Eight or nine miles away, and over a thousand feet lower, the last tin roofs of Addis flash a dazzling heliograph in the snipe-bogs beyond the airport. Between these two points, spaced out along the broad bands of tarmac at regular intervals, are the varied elements of the European town: the cosy stone bungalows of foreign advisers; brick-and-glass schools; a severely functional opera house; a lavishly gilded cathedral of St George; the modest palaces of the royal family, including the Emperor's Ghibbi (or palace) at whose gates a pair of mangy lions are still symbolically chained today, just as they were once chained by the tented palace of Prester John; and lastly, on the farthest periphery of the town, the palatial embassies of foreign powers.

In contrast to the town, the village of Addis is earthily picturesque. The outlines of shack and mud-hut are diffused by a green mist of eucalyptus trees; the wood-smoke seeps from the apertures in the roof; the red soil is fragrant with a pot-pourri of fallen leaves. Along a forest path trudge Galla women laboriously fetching water from the local stream in three-handled pitchers. Others squat outside their huts on a packing-case while someone plaits and butters their hair. And above the hurly-burly of the traffic in the main road a hundred yards away is heard the thin piping of the flute, and the insistent beat of the wedding drum.

The metalled roads which town and village hold in common present a lively scene. Along these roads the grave young *évolués* and debonair foreign advisers bowl along in their official cars. Pedestrians, some driving cattle, spill out into the streets. Horse-drawn gharries, and motor gharries (a sort of scooter–rickshaw) weave among them like slalom-racers.

For the coming Jubilee, triumphal arches had been erected along the processional route and huge, gold-lettered greetings in Amharic hung across the streets like a mayoral chain. Pictures of the Emperor, stylized copies of the official photographs, beckoned from every wall.

My own feelings about the coming Jubilee were ambivalent. I could not help regarding it as an obstacle between myself and the Mountain; my letters of introduction were useless at a time like this. At the same time I hoped that the festivities might prove to be in the exotic tradition of the Abyssinia described by Evelyn Waugh; as a tourist I was shamelessly in search of the exotic.

There were surprisingly few tourists in Addis for the Jubilee. Most of the visitors were foreign journalists. For them this excursion was, I suppose, a pleasant holiday from the cold war in the Middle East where they were based. At any rate, they seemed contented enough at the official openings of schools and hotels, the presentations of gifts to His Imperial Majesty, and other events heralding the Jubilee ceremonies themselves.

For myself I found that these official ceremonies were the least interesting aspect of life in Addis. Any hopes I might have had of two exotic weeks of festivities were, I could see from the preparations, doomed to disappointment. Despite the Jubilee, however, I saw a good deal of the town and village of Addis; this was, as I have said, joyously bizarre. And most evenings, in one way or another, I managed to escape the official receptions and strike out on my own.

One evening I wandered off to the old ghibbi to the east of the town. It was a shaggy complex of buildings sprawling across a hillside of brown grass. Around the precincts the juniper trees, indigenous to Ethiopia but almost ousted by the imported eucalyptus, still hung in tattered green clumps. There was an air of melancholy about these seedy junipers,

Ambas near Adowa seen on my way from Asmara to Gondar. This was the graveyard for 5,000 Italians and allies crushed by Menelik at the Battle of Adowa in 1896. In 1935–6 the Italians paid off the score and conquered Ethiopia.

'You'll be loaded down with luxuries like mosquito-nets, camp-beds, tents and you'll probably have a private army to guard you. Frankly I prefer to travel light. You too?' I had to confess that to me the prospect of such luxuries sounded quite delightful.

and about the dusty mews and stables which have been deserted since the new ghibbi was built after the war. I peered into the great barn-like structure which served as a banqueting-hall; here a thousand are said to have sat at table when Menelik gave the ceremonial raw-meat feast at Easter to end the Lenten fast (see illustration on pp 166–7), but today it was forlorn and empty, and an odour of rottenness and decay clung to the rough stone walls and rafters. I shivered, and looked back almost nostalgically to the red plush and the healthy Trust House atmosphere of the new ghibbi.

When I emerged a change had come over the small band of retainers and beggars that hovered about the precincts. They formed up in a ragged line along the path to the ghibbi, and presently a discreet black Rolls-Royce, distinguished only by its lack of number plates, came creeping up this avenue of tattered old men, each of whom prostrated himself to the ground as it passed. I thought of the way a summer wind blows up an avenue of cypresses, bowing each in turn. When the Rolls-Royce reached me I found myself facing no less a man than the Emperor.

At the official ceremonies I had seen him often enough at close quarters (unlike most absolute monarchs, he seems to rely on his personal sacrosanctity and eschews a proper bodyguard); I had even shaken his hand and murmured my respects to him in French at an official reception. But those had been mechanical enough affairs, which had left me unmoved. Here in the melancholy desolation of the old ghibbi, I found that the sight of the Emperor's diminutive but

patriarchal figure – he has a bushy beard, noble Levantine features, and above all the fierce, unflinching eyes of a visionary – evoked in me a feeling close to religious awe. It was a solemn thought to consider how much his country owed to him.

Thursday was Jubilee-day according to the Ethiopian calendar. (It was the day after Jubilee-day according to the Georgian calendar, but no one worried.) The ceremonies proved to be no more nor less interesting than I had anticipated from the preparations.

A vast marquee had been erected on one side of the cathedral of St George. Here the Emperor, dressed in the uniform of a European Field-Marshal, sat among his peers; they wore anonymous European dress. In tier after tier of wooden seats sat those European residents who had been favoured with seats; they were rather more excitingly dressed. The church service, which was largely invisible to the congregation, was soon over. It was followed by a State drive. The spectators lining the streets were colourful enough, though I would have preferred to see them animated, not penned in like sheep at a market. The Emperor's coach (a green landau made in Belgium) was followed by a cortège of the discreet black cars that find favour with royalty. It was hardly a thrilling occasion.

At various times since my arrival I had felt a sense of frustration over the lack of progress in the search for the Mountain. This feeling reached a climax on the night of the Jubilee. The prospect of further receptions, military parades, displays of traditional dancing, was far from inviting. I wished with all my heart that I could think of some way of escaping them.

Next morning this wish seemed ironic enough. I awoke feeling exceedingly unwell; a glance in the mirror revealed that my eyes had taken on a hideous yellow tinge. My temperature climbed rapidly; by evening I was diagnosed as a quite severe case of jaundice. There was no question of waiting to attend the festivities. For three days I languished, with the jaundice inexorably gaining ground. On the fourth I was rescued by two good Samaritans, Ann and Robby Roberts, who scooped me up in an ambulance and drove me away to their palatial house in the suburbs. 'Come and stay with us till you're better.'

Crumpets with the Governor

While I lay weak and yellow with jaundice in the Roberts' elegant nursery in a suburb of Addis, the tide of events was at last moving in the direction of the Mountain.

From Amaha Kassa, the young Ethiopian recommended to me by the Byzantinist, I received a cheerful letter of support. As soon as I was well I must come and meet the Governor-General of Gondar and together they could arrange my expedition. From Stephen Wright, another ally recommended by the Byzantinist, I received a personal visit.

Stephen Wright was a remarkable English scholar and traveller who now worked in the Ministry of Education. In the last six or seven years, however, he had travelled very widely across the virtually unmapped and unexplored plateau that runs for hundreds of miles to the north of Addis. He would know better than anyone the conditions in the interior, and how I should best prepare myself for my journey. He might even (a horrid thought), have already visited the Mountain himself.

He proved to know much of the literature about the Mountain. But I was relieved to hear he only knew dimly of its whereabouts. 'There's a place called Wachni,' he said, 'to the west of Gondar, about three days by mule towards the low country.' I told him that I believed the Mountain lay to the south-east. 'I know,' he replied, 'that's what Bruce says, but I've never been there.'

He generously added that he would help me to get there as far as he was able. I must come over when I had recovered and talk over the details of the trip. Of course if the Governor-General, Asserate Kassa (who was Amaha's uncle), was backing me I would be well looked after. He was always very generous to Englishmen. 'Too generous,' he added with a laugh. 'You'll be loaded down with luxuries like mosquito-nets, camp-beds, tents and you'll probably have a private army to guard you. Frankly I prefer to travel light. You too?' I had to confess that to me the prospect of such luxuries sounded quite delightful.

The first step to be taken now that I had more or less recovered was to go and see Amaha Kassa. A few days later I found myself taking a motor gharry – the horse-drawn gharry

PRECEDING PAGE AND LEFT: *the Simien mountains (photographed in 1998) whose summit, Ras Dasha, (on the sky-line on p. 23), falls little short of 15,000 feet. On my way to Gondar I crossed the Simien in a lorry. After the heat of the plain, the Alpine meadows made me blink.*

is a little cheaper but may take more than an hour to cross from one end of Addis to the other – out to Amaha's house in the suburbs. Like the foreign diplomats, the richer Ethiopians have their houses some miles from the town centre. After a long, and somewhat perilous, journey inside the cab of the scooter-taxi, we arrived at a modest European-style house on the edge of a great forest of blue gums.

Amaha had invited along Colonel Shifferaw of Gondar who was an expert on the topography of the area. Over their whiskies we discussed the first problem – how to find the Mountain. Stephen Wright's view was that the prison for the Princes was west of Gondar; at any rate there was a mountain called Wachni three days to the west. The Colonel insisted it was to the east of Gondar. 'I know of two Wehnis,' he said, 'and both are to the east. One's pretty near the motor-road, so you could do it in a day from Gondar. I went there during the war when I was fighting with the patriots. The other Wehni must be about three days' journey by mule into the mountains of Belesa. I haven't been there myself, but I know it was one of the patriot strongholds. The Italians never penetrated there.'

'Excellent.' I said, 'I shouldn't like any European to have been there before me. The wilder and the more remote the place, the better.'

'Be careful, Tom,' said Amaha grinning. 'If your Mountain is in too wild a place you may not be allowed to go there. It may be too dangerous. But we shall see. Maybe Colonel Shifferaw will come and defend you from the bandits.'

The trouble with Amaha was that I never felt entirely sure when he was joking. At any rate the main problem had been swiftly resolved. There were only three Mountains known, one of which must surely be the right one. If necessary I could visit all three.

The secondary problem of how to get there was settled less satisfactorily. Amaha advised me not to worry. He was sure that the Governor-General – his powerful uncle, Asserate Kassa – would be willing to help me get my expedition together. I might even be invited to stay in his palace. Amaha loyally arranged for me to meet the Governor-General. On this meeting depended much of the success of my expedition to the Mountain. On the day appointed for my interview I dressed in my now discredited dark suit (I had fondly imagined that Addis would be too hot for a charcoal worsted suit, and had brought only an old one which proved infinitely dowdy in the eyes of the smart young set) and boldly hired a taxi to take me to the Governor's ghibbi. The price was ruinous but this was, I felt, an investment. Asserate Kassa must not feel that his future guest was an indigent undergraduate. 'Act the aristocrat,' were the Byzantinist's last words; 'the Ethiopians are traditionalists. They respect money, and they respect breeding. Make them feel you've plenty of both.' But I could not persuade myself, as I rode along in the taxi in my crumpled and much darned suit, wondering whether I need tip the driver, that I was the picture of the rich milord. I paid off the taxi, rang the bell beside the slate-blue front door, and no sabanya or feudal retainer answered the door – Asserate Kassa himself came to let me in.

In my imagination I had pictured him as an older version of Amaha – with a yellow cast of complexion, strongly Semitic features, and the sort of crisp black hair that seems specially characteristic of Ethiopia. But Asserate Kassa was of a different type altogether. In the first place he was very tall – the tallest Amhara I saw with the exception of the Emperor's personal bodyguard, a giant of a man who accompanied him on official occasions. At the same time he was not tall-and-spindly like a Somali; indeed he was so well-proportioned that his great height was not immediately apparent. His features again were utterly unlike Amaha's or indeed those of any members of the ruling families that I had seen. They were not Semitic at all, but cast in the strong regular mould that is sometimes called typical of English aristocrats. A square chin, straight nose and high forehead were the essential ingredients of this, and the approach of baldness gave a still more European look to an already European face; baldness is almost unknown among Ethiopians. The only purely African element in his face and the one which made him, to my mind, supremely good-looking, was his unusually full-blooded, black-treacle complexion.

Asserate Kassa was the fourth son of Ras Kassa. His father had looked like becoming Regent on the deposition of Lij Yasu, Menelik's grandson, in 1916. But the council of nobles who deposed Lij Yasu has apparently preferred a less controversial candidate, his second cousin Ras Tafari, though the latter's claim to the throne was poorer than Ras Kassa's. So Ras Tafari became Regent and eventually succeeded to the throne. He is now the Emperor Haile Selassie. Ras Kassa remained an important Governor, and his duties included the office of jailer to Lij Yasu till his escape in 1932. With his youngest son, Asserate Kassa, he accompanied the Emperor in the years of exile in England. His three elder sons, one of whom was Amaha's father, were murdered by the Italians in 1937, so Asserate Kassa was now the only surviving son.

Asserate Kassa now led me down a panelled corridor to the drawing-room. The room was decorated in conventional European good taste, with an Empire wall-paper and Regency furniture. 'Shall we have some tea?' he said cordially. He pressed an ivory bell-push. 'I think there are crumpets today.' We chatted about food and furniture till the tea things were brought in on a tray by a servant. Then as politely as I could I turned the conversation from crumpets to Gondar and the Mountain.

Behind me in a Sheraton cabinet I had observed the original six volumes of Bruce's *Travels*, the principal source I was following, as well as numerous other books on Ethiopia from the sixteenth century till the present day. I asked my host what he thought of James Bruce and his controversial works. Asserate Kassa affected to admire him as much as I did, but did not, however, give the impression of having read them very closely. Though the Governor of Gondar, he had barely heard of the Mountain, and had much less definite views on its whereabouts than Colonel Shifferaw. 'Don't worry, you will find it,' he said, obviously ill at ease. 'Wait till you get to Gondar.' I could not press him further.

For the next twenty minutes we talked of England; of the season and Ascot; of Oxford; of Henley and rowing; of the House of Lords. Asserate Kassa was very curious to know details. I answered his cross-examination as best as I could, though in fact painfully ignorant of these matters. He seemed hardly satisfied, even when the tea things were cleared away and the light was already fading outside. He still gave no sign of wishing to help me in my expedition. I returned for the third time to the real purpose of my visit. He did not appear to be listening. Instead he took out a large red volume from the bookshelf, and began to read it with his back to me. 'How old are you?' he said suddenly, rather to my alarm. 'Are you Thomas Frank Dermot, born 1933?' I confessed I was. His manner changed abruptly. 'Well, of course I will help you.' He wrote a letter of introduction to the Director-General of Gondar, another for the palace major-domo, a certain Fitarawi Gabremariam. I made what I hoped was a suitable expression of thanks and shortly afterwards said good-bye to him.

He had told his driver to drop me back in the town centre and we were soon sweeping away in his Mercedes from the Kassa Ghibbi. I was delighted to get the letters, of course, which should help me enormously. But I confess I was puzzled at the course of our interview. I had expected my familiarity with Ethiopian history to be examined, not my familiarity with the nuances of the London season. Then as the Mercedes turned out of the Kassa compound I remembered the words of the Byzantinist. The large red volume which had seemed so irrelevant to the occasion yet which had seemed to weigh so heavily in my favour – I could guess what it was now. Unimpressed by my appearance and my answers he had been looking me up in Debrett.

With the letters of introduction from Asserate Kassa, I was finally ready to leave for Gondar. Next day I flew northwards to Asmara. From there I visited the pagan obelisks of Axum – relics of Sheba's Ethiopia – and the crown of King Theodore, who killed himself when the British invaded Abyssinia in 1867–8. We also glimpsed the ambas near Adowa, where the Italian army was crushed by Menelik in 1896.

A week later I found myself in the cab of a petrol truck approaching the great mountain barrier of the Simien, the last obstacle before Gondar. Till this moment I had thought that the road that spirals up from Kotor to Cetinje in Montenegro the most spectacular in the world. It could not compare with this road over the Simien, built by Fascist engineers after the Italian conquest of Ethiopia in 1935–6. In the first place we left behind us a dry, dun-coloured jungle of pampas grass, and cobweb-like acacias, and huge cowslips, and a sort of thorn tree with the bright sheen of aluminium; and we rose into an Alpine land of black rock with splashing streams, cascades of wild vines and convolvulus, and white-

winged eagles. Then there was the road itself. For the last ten miles the Italian engineers had literally carved a way up the mountain wall, in a breath-taking series of arabesques. No expense had been spared to make this what the pre-war Italian guide-book called 'la piu grandiosa realizzazione de l'Impero' ('The empire's grandest project'). There were even massive drinking fountains at the side of the road, carved in a Fascist baroque style, with allegorical figures representing Italy and Africa. And near the summit of the pass was a grandiose war memorial, like the entrance gates of a Scottish baronial castle, carrying the proud legend: 'Non siamo morte in vano' ('We have not died in vain'). The words did not somehow seem ironical here. The magnificent road which the Italian workmen had died in making was today, unlike many Italian projects in the country, more useful than ever.

It was dusk when we reached the plateau. We had climbed for three solid hours and were now 8,000 feet higher. Ahead of us stretched a generous prospect of green meadows dotted with feathery acacias. After the heat and tumult of the afternoon the sight made one blink. There was a stylized, tapestry-like quality to the landscape. It was no surprise when a gazelle, dappled grey in the twilight, bounded from a mossy bank on the left and stood wide-eyed to watch us pass.

I spent that night in the cab of the lorry, while the driver slept in a shack at the side of the road. Next morning we were off before dawn.

Bruce had written: 'We were gratified at last by the sight of Gondar, according to my computation about ten miles distant. The King's Palace (at least the tower of it) is distinctly seen, but none of the other houses, which are covered by a multitude of wanzey trees.' This had etched a clear picture in my mind, though I did not doubt that it would have little in common with a first view of Gondar today. But in fact Bruce's picture was accurate enough.

At eight-thirty, with the long shadows of the morning sun overhanging the valley, we saw Gondar in the distance – a black cloud of trees against the brown mountainside, with the top of a tower peering superciliously over them.

Half an hour later we had crossed the river Angareb and were trundling down an avenue of wanzey trees towards the King's palace.

At eight-thirty, with the long shadows of the
morning sun overhanging the valley, we saw Gondar
in the distance – a black cloud of trees against the
brown mountainside, with the top of a tower peering
superciliously over them.

The modern city of Gondar (photographed in 1998)
with the seventeenth-century palace of King Facilidas
(INSET, LEFT) and other palaces on the crown of the
hill. Soon after 1632, Facilidas chose Mount Wehni
as the third prison mountain.

Gondar

Dismal are the examples among the Barbarians where there are no laws of succession ... What ruined the family of the Caesars? What the Roman Empire? The ancient Kings of Abyssinia, to rid themselves of such Wars, were wont to shut up their brothers in safe custody where they might abide unknown to turbulent spirits ... and yet be ready to supply the want of the sucessors.

Jerome Ludolf: *History of Ethiopia, 1681*

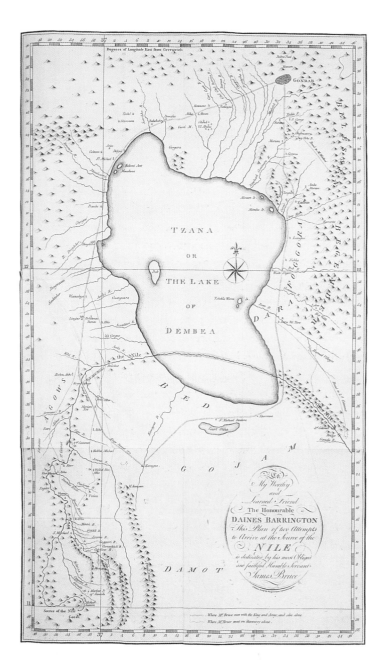

Before I had left Addis I had been given a letter by Asserate Kassa to deliver to his vizier at Gondar, a certain Fitarawi Woldemariam. When I reached Gondar I found him outside the Governor's palace, an old man, dressed in a shabby, brown pinstripe suit, crowned with a battered topee. At first he asked impatiently what I wanted of him; he was taking his son to hospital and could not delay. But after he had read the Governor-General's letter his manner changed abruptly. He shook my hand cordially and messengers were sent hurrying to alert the guardian of the ghibbi guest-house. He offered me a cup of milkless tea meanwhile. Of course he would have met me himself if he had known. Where was my car? 'Gone,' I said airily, hoping that the news of my arrival by lorry would not reach his ears. 'I sent it back.'

The guest-house was set in a grove of pepper-trees and proved as delectable as its surroundings. After two nights and days in the lorry I revelled at the thought of the endless hot baths offered by its immersion heater, the velvet-covered armchairs in the little parlour off the dining-room, and the succession of bountiful meals offered by Tafara, the guardian of the guest-house. There was *vitello arrosto*, he announced for lunch, with French beans and fried potatoes, followed by fruit salad. Would I drink wine with the meal – he could offer Chianti or White Bordeaux – or did I prefer beer at lunch? Tafara seemed as excited by the prospect of serving these delicacies as I was at the prospect of eating them; presumably guests were rare. Lunch, when it arrived from the palace kitchens, was no disappointment. The excellent meal was served in state. I lunched alone at a great

mahogany table loaded with silver, and by my plate was a small posy of pinks and snapdragons, set in a cluster of fern.

From the dining-room windows the valley to the east of Gondar was plainly visible, spread out under the hot light of noon like a piece of rough material discoloured in places. Beyond our grove of pepper-trees the fields began, brown ploughland interspersed with patches of maize and wheat stubble, each stubble field pocked with a threshing circle. There were a few villages of circular tukal-huts, planted like fungi in the cracks of the plain where there were streams. Beyond the plain rose the corrugated façade of a mountain range, its grey limestone surface uncannily like weathered stucco. In the crisp light of the African noon the wall of rock looked hardly five miles off, though my map made it nearer fifteen. These were the mountains of Belesa. Somewhere beyond them to the east, if Bruce's sketch map was to be trusted, lay the Mountain of the Princes.

After a rest in my bedroom, whose balcony enjoyed the same dreamlike view of plain and mountain, I took a stroll down to the city itself. My letter of recommendation to Colonel Tamarat, the Director-General, crackled reassuringly in my inside pocket; the sun's heat by three-thirty was hot without being overpowering; the cicadas sang soothingly in the gum-trees lining the dusty street. I felt unusually at peace with the world. My only regret was that I had failed to get my shoes mended in Addis, and the stony surface of the decaying tarmac roads made walking rather painful. No doubt I could have a new pair made locally. For the present I stuffed the soles with newspaper and hobbled on towards the imperial city whose great battlemented walls were already visible beyond the crumbling stucco houses of the Italian town.

Gondar became the capital of the Empire in 1632, and remained so for nearly two hundred years. It was founded by King Facilidas. The situation when he ascended the throne had been critical, the Moslem wars of 1527–43 having almost totally destroyed the medieval Christian civilization; and the Turks had robbed Ethiopia of her outlet to the Red Sea. Since then the king and his followers had led a semi-nomadic life, setting up court wherever the king halted. He had a summer camp on Lake Tana, and a winter camp in the foothills to the east of Gondar; but mostly he lived in a tent travelling from one village to another administering his territory. There was no administrative capital, so no architecture in dressed stone or brick except the one extraordinary palace at Gorgora the Jesuits built King Suseneyos in 1614, shortly before they were expelled, its baroque splendour soon buried in the jungle-growth of papyrus and liana.

The country which had been divided over the religious controversy under his predecessor was now united by Facilidas. The monophysite faith was re-adopted as the universal religion and the remaining Catholics were expelled or put to death. Facilidas thus restored the power of the monarchy as well as the unity of his people. The monarchy depended on the Church for its strength. But the problem of the princes was harder to solve. In the Abyssinian system all the King's male blood relations, whether 'legitimate' or the fruit of a less permanent union, had some claim to the throne. There was no heir who automatically succeeded. A successor was normally nominated by the King and the Court, but, as there were often as many as fifty or more candidates, the King's choice was apt to arouse dissension. Princes not chosen by the King were often the focus of revolt; and the execution of sixty princes in the previous reign had not solved the problem, but merely exacerbated it.

Facilidas decided to solve the problem in a more subtle way than by the indiscriminate slaughter of his relations. The heir to the throne would naturally remain in Gondar ready to be crowned if anything should happen to the King, but the other prospective heirs were to be removed from circulation. Facilidas decided on the prison-mountain of Wehni as a suitable place for them; it was near Gondar and quite escape-proof. Provided the Governor of the Mountain was faithful to the King, life at Court could continue undisturbed.

The prisoners on the mountain lived a grim life. Facilidas, Bruce records, set aside a mere 250 ounces of gold for their maintenance, and provided 750 cloaks to clothe them and their guards. But the Governor of the Mountain tended to embezzle even this meagre allowance. Food was often scarce; the cistern on the summit of the Mountain very soon ran dry and water had to be laboriously carried jug by jug to the summit; no visitors were admitted to break the monotony of the princes' days. If letters were delivered at all they were examined for signs of plans to escape; and for these there were severe penalties – mutilation or even death. 'Tekla Georghis,' the Royal Chronicle says, 'lived in fear that they would cut off his hands and his feet and pluck out his eyes ... but God preserved him as he preserved Joseph from Pharaoh and Daniel from the wrath of lions.' Some of his companions were not so fortunate.

Despite the punishments imposed, there were many attempts at escape. One prisoner, for example, camouflaged himself with a large bush and crept from the summit like Macduff's soldiers impersonating Birnam Wood. Sadly the bush was only too obvious as it descended the mountain and the ingenious prince was recaptured. Another, Bacuffa the Inexorable, ran away in the confusion caused by the election to the throne of one of his colleagues. He was helped by his sister who had somehow got access to the Mountain. But

Bacuffa was recaptured and returned minus the tip of his nose, since mutilation was supposed to debar a prince from the succession. Bacuffa nevertheless became King in 1721. Usually escapes were made by bribing the guards, but none of the escapers succeeded in reaching Gondar.

Yet the princes' lot had its compensations. In previous reigns they might be executed as a precautionary measure. Now, if they accepted their fate with resignation, they could be ignored. Johannes, chosen to succeed his nephew in 1682 and brought to the capital to be crowned, even preferred the ascetic life on the Mountain to the luxury of Gondar. He demurred at the prospect of leading an army in battle, and taking a young princess as his wife. He wept, we are told, hid himself, and begged to be taken back to the Mountain. This attitude was considered too perverse. Johannes was poisoned at one of the sumptuous breakfasts enjoyed at Gondar, and a more suitable candidate brought from Wehni.

There was also the unique occasion when the whole body of princes were offered their freedom and voted to remain. King Yasous (or Joshua),

Seventeenth-century palace of King Yasous, grandson of King Facilidas. He offered the princes their freedom. But they voted to stay locked up on the Mountain.

grandson of Facilidas, had camped with his whole army at the foot of the Mountain, and sent for the Governor, who was told that all the prisoners must be released and that he would be compensated for the loss of his revenue. But the prisoners, on being allowed to descend and given the good news, went in a deputation to the King. They thanked him for his magnanimity, they begged him not to be angry – but they could never agree, they insisted, to the order for their release. They felt it would be fatal to the stability of the empire, and would consider acceptance of the order an act of treason to their sovereign. So with one accord they returned voluntarily to their prison. This was the story, at least, that was told to James Bruce by King Teklahaimanot who reigned in the following century.

It is to Bruce that we owe most of our knowledge of the history of this period. He arrived in Gondar in 1770, nearly 150 years after Facilidas had built the first great palace there and made it his capital. The storm was already gathering which would culminate in the destruction of the city and the

dissolution of the empire. But the Court still lived in habitual splendour. The old magnificence lingered; the rituals of the hunt and the rites of the Church were respected as solemnly as ever. Court life was as stiff and as stylized as under any of the Kings, and the buildings of Gondar as formidable.

'The King's house at Gondar,' Bruce relates, 'stands in the middle of a square court. In the midst of it is a square tower, in which there are many noble apartments. A strong double wall surrounds it, and this is joined by a platform roof; loopholes are disposed all round. The whole tower and wall is built of stone and lime ... all the apartments are magnificently lined and furnished .... They have likewise magnificent names.'

It was here that Bruce had his first audience with Teklahaimanot. 'The King was seated upon the throne, very richly dressed in brocade, a very fine muslin web wrapt loosely about him, so as to hang in plaits, and in some parts to show and in others to conceal the flowers of the cloth of gold of which his waistcoat was composed. His hair was loose, combed out at full length, and a fork made of rhinoceros horn with a gold head upon it stuck through his hair; he was all perfumed with rose water, and two people stood at opposite sides each of them with a silver bottle full of it...' Bruce, like other visitors, was duly doused with it.

The Englishman was soon on excellent terms with the King and his family. Considered a 'King's stranger', a guest of the country, he was given a country house and sinecure of being one of the six Baalomal or Gentlemen of the Bedchamber. His linguistic gifts (he

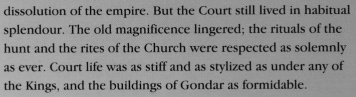

spoke eight languages, according to his own account, and knew eleven) and haughty bearing distinguished him at once from previous European visitors – from Greece and Armenia. His excellence as a rider and shot were sources of wonder. They had never seen a double-barrelled gun before and 'did not know that its effect was limited to two discharges but thought that it might be fired on to infinity'. Inevitably he was a great success with the ladies of the Court – 'having an accidental knack,' he says, 'which is not a trifle, of putting on the dress and speaking the language easily, I cultivated with the utmost assiduity the friendship of the fair sex'.

Gondar did not always adhere to European conventions in the treatment of guests. During the rainy season when Bruce had retired to his room, he would suddenly hear four or five hundred people 'roaring and crying as if they would that moment expire'. He would send a soldier to see what was the matter with them, imagining there had been a fight. But the reply came back: nothing was the matter with any of them: 'they had seen me,' Bruce says, 'retire to my room and had come to do me honour before the people for fear I should be melancholy by being too quiet alone. The violent anger which this did often put me into did not fail to be punctually reported to the King at which he would laugh heartily; and he himself was often hid not far off, for the sake of being a spectator of my hearty displeasure.'

Life at the Abyssinian Court, which Bruce was in a unique position to observe, owed a great debt to the Osmanli Sultans. Turkish pavilions lined with Eastern silks grew ever more popular, while courtiers were dressed in the rich brocades of Turkish fashion. As for the King he modelled himself on the Sultan. He was, we are told, all-powerful and a law to himself. But the Abyssinian copy of Turkish manners sometimes verged on parody. When the King entered the throne-room in the morning he rode in on his royal mule, considering it beneath his dignity to walk even in his own palace. When he dispensed justice he had to sit behind an arras: invisibly he presided over the court and sent his verdict through a special chamberlain. At Gondar there was a touch of burlesque in even the most solemn rituals.

Despite the successful working of the Mountain the Abyssinian civilization had become unstable by the time of Bruce. There was a flavour of unreality, an ominous dream-like quality about Court life at Gondar. 'Do you in Europe see the same face of the moon as we?' asked the King, when Bruce had his first interview. At any moment, it seemed, the whole fabric, towers, palaces and all might vanish into thin air. The end, in fact, came very quickly. The King's chief minister, Ras Michael, who 'rolls up lead balls for a gun and hurls them on the face of the Enemy', as the Chronicle says, seized power. The King became a king only in name. Civil

war broke out. The old idea of the sanctity of the King's person was forgotten. He himself had to fly from Gondar. Within a year of Bruce's departure from the country the whole world of Gondar had collapsed and the country had relapsed into a state of tribal anarchy.

Yet strangely the prisoners on the Mountain did not perish in the holocaust. The natural temptation was to liquidate them, as the four hundred princes on Debra Damo had been liquidated at the beginning of the first great civil wars of the ninth century. This we know did not happen on Wehni. Ras Michael proposed it: he told the council that his familiar, the archangel Michael, had suggested to him in a dream that they should surprise the Mountain on their return to Gondar and put the prisoners to the sword. For once the King and the Court withstood him, perhaps recognizing that the present crisis could not be laid at the prisoners' door, and that by their imprisonment they had been the faithful safeguard of the Gondar regime until Gondar itself had been abandoned. This time the enemy had not been the King's turbulent relations but the feudal chiefs. So the prisoners were allowed to disperse and the last Rip Van Winkle climbed down the steep staircase to the world he had left half a century before.

Today, as I found at my first visit to the imperial city, the five castles (really fortified palaces) of Gondar still rise grandly from their pleasure-gardens. I passed through the Gate of the Judges, the principal gateway in the curtain wall enclosing the palaces. Ahead of me stretched a prospect of trim lawns, flowering terraces, and courtyards neatly adorned with wanzey trees – from these rose the five palaces. As they had been recently cleaned and restored they lacked the glamour of decay; at the same time they were just as imposing as I had imagined from Bruce's descriptions.

The palace of Facilidas (or Fasil Ghibbi) is the largest of all the palaces. It would be perverse not to find it the most impressive. The crenellated tower rises to four stories; five pepper-pot turrets rear up like minarets; the honey-coloured limestone façade is pierced with tall round-headed windows, lined with blocks of violet tufa and dressed with tufa capitals. At its side are two lesser palaces – a Chancellery and a Library. To the east lies the palace of King Yasous. Down a flight of steps beyond lurks the palace of Bacuffa. At the

LEFT: *Seventeenth-century palace and library of King Johannes.*
CENTRE: *Seventeenth-century palace of King Facilidas comparing a contemporary manuscript with a photograph of the 1960s.* FAR RIGHT: *Eighteenth-century palace of King Bacuffa, who escaped from the Mountain, and Queen Mentuab.*

northernmost extent of the great curtain wall lies the palace of Mentuab, who was Queen Mother in Bruce's time. Its square façade is inlaid with curious niches of tufa. Finally, dotted among the palaces are what remains of the pavilions and kiosks of the imperial city – the House of Lions, the House of the Singer of King David – while close by, in a cascade of creeper, are the ruins of the Church of Noah's Ark.

The five palaces of Gondar were, I found, imposing without being at all picturesque. On the same day as I first entered the imperial city I visited two other palaces beyond its walls. Here I found the picturesque decay that Gondar itself had lacked. In the valley of the river Caa, among a grove of dusty junipers, lies the summer palace of Facilidas, and a mile or two beyond the summer palace is the palace of Cusquam, built by Queen Mentuab, which was Bruce's eventual refuge from the increasing coarseness and savagery of the Court of Gondar. It marks the final

stage of the Gondarin style of architecture.

Like the main palaces of Gondar Cusquam is surrounded by a curtain wall; but this has crumbled away on the western side so that one can simply step inside the courtyard. From the single shattered turret liana hangs in emerald swags; the great stone archways are half strangled with convolvulus; while a jungle-growth of grawa and gotom trees has obscured the long palace-walks and the high, stone terraces. Like the palace of Mentuab it has a Renaissance flavour. Here are the pepper-pot tower and the long, unvaulted halls of the earlier buildings, probably owing their inspiration to the mud palaces of South Arabia; but here also are pink niches of tufa inlaid into the façade, and heraldic motives – a lion and an elephant, an orb and a Maltese cross.

My letter of introduction to Colonel Tamarat bore fruit with remarkable, indeed with alarming speed. As I dined in the guest-house on my first evening in Gondar, the telephone rang sharply. 'Colonello c'e,' announced Tafara. I took up the receiver, expecting to hear a long tale of delay and prevarication. By now I was quite accustomed to the slow tempo of provincial life, and looked forward to a leisurely week of preparations. 'Don't worry,' I began, 'I know these things take time to arrange.' Colonel Tamarat cut me short. 'Everything is arranged already, Mr Pakenham. You

will start tomorrow morning as soon as it is light.' Considerably unnerved I walked down to his office after dinner to learn the details of my expedition.

Colonel Tamarat was tall, military and spoke English like a Frenchman. He had been educated at St Cyr. He gave me a chair opposite him and waved the mass of litigants out of the room. 'Well, Mr Pakenham, everything is arranged just as His Excellency the Governor-General suggested. The Governor of Belesa, who is in Gondar this week, will accompany you; he has his own escort and I will give you some soldiers as well. I will send a boy from the ghibbi to be your own servant. And I will arrange for a young police lieutenant to go with you as interpreter. Does this suit you?'

I thanked him warmly. Despite Stephen Wright's warning about travelling light, I felt my expedition in such royal style would have far better chances of success. 'I will introduce you to the Governor of Belesa,' continued Colonel Tamarat. 'No doubt he has planned your route already.' He pressed a buzzer on his desk and a servant came in, bowed, disappeared, reappeared with a young man in military uniform and Sam Browne belt, bowed and disappeared again. The young man was the Governor of Belesa.

We shook hands. He cannot have been much more than thirty, but was an exceptionally impressive figure among a people whose grave and stolid dignity is remarkable. I looked forward to some interesting discussions through the medium of our interpreter. The Governor, though of the post-Italian generation, spoke little or no English. For the moment, Colonel Tamarat obligingly interpreted for us.

The second Mountain, the one that Colonel Shifferaw had described as farthest from the road, was the one that the Governor took to be the prison-mountain of the Princes. The other Wehni, he insisted, had been just a casual prison of no historical importance. This was the local tradition. I told him that Bruce's map showed the Mountain to be north-east of Enfras on Lake Tana. 'That is right,' the Governor replied. Enfras was now of little importance and we could bypass it, but the Mountain was certainly north-east of it. 'And is it hard to get up?' asked Colonel Tamarat, grinning. 'Will you need ropes to climb it?' To this question the Governor was less quick to reply. 'He does not think so; yet he is not sure. You had better take some extra ropes.' 'Hasn't he been there himself?' I asked anxiously. To this Colonel Tamarat replied, 'Don't worry, you will find it, I am sure. But whether you will be able to climb up or not we cannot tell.' On this enigmatic note our little conference ended.

Chapter Two

At Selim I still was encompassed by the scenes and the sounds of familiar life; the din of the busy world still vexed and cheered me; yet whenever I chose to look southward, I saw the Otttoman's fortress high over the vale of the Danube. I had come as it were to the end of wheel-going Europe, and now my eyes would see the splendour and havoc of the East.

Kinglake: *Eothen*

To the Mountain

In a moment we would stand, like Kinglake, at the frontiers of the wheel-going world. Behind us would be the Ethiopia of the motor-road; the progressive, secure Ethiopia of Haile Selassie; ahead the unchanging, exotic, perhaps even perilous Ethiopia of Prester John. The ghibbi truck loaded with my escort clattered into Tuesday Market and we had reached the frontier.

It was nine o'clock in the morning and the fields were still dewy around us. We jumped down from the truck – myself, the Governor of Belesa, the police captain, Tafara (who had obtained permission to accompany me on the expedition) and twelve armed retainers of the Governor's. Most of these were roughly dressed and barefooted.

The village of Tuesday Market, whose name aptly described it, lay directly to the west of our goal, so the Governor assured me. From here the Debra Tabor road ran southwards, skirting the great bulk of the Belesa plateau. To follow the road any longer would bring us no nearer the Mountain, so he had arranged for his escort to meet us here, bringing with them mules for us to ride and pack-mules to carry the provisions and camping equipment. 'Some pack-mules are here already; the rest will be here any moment,' said the Governor through the medium of Teshome, the police captain. I had my own views about the likelihood of their being punctual, but I was happy to wait and see. I was in no particular hurry to entrust myself to the caprices of a mule and leave the grateful shade of Tuesday Market.

Today was Tuesday. Already the first market-goers were beginning to filter into the compound between the huts on whose hard-baked mud floor the wooden frames of stalls were being set up. I sat under the shade of a spreading bamboula tree, planted in the middle of the village compound like a chestnut on an English village green, and watched the market slowly take shape, as the shadows shortened and the day wore on, and still the mules did not come.

About twelve o'clock Tafara called to me to come to a tukul-hut where lunch was prepared. I was overwhelmed by what I found in the hut. Its earth floor had been covered by a rich Indian carpet; a large canteen of silver was half unpacked in one corner; a packing-case labelled Pernod Fils

was spread with Irish linen, and a place for me already laid; while in a canvas bucket a bottle of Moselle was cooling; and what was perhaps the rarest delicacy of all in a tropical country, a pound of fresh Asmara butter which Tafara had brought in a marmalade-pot. 'Lunch is served,' Tafara announced, grinning with pleasure at my astonishment. 'Will you wait till the wine is cool or drink it now?' I drank it then, filling my glass often as I ate the roasted veal that an hour before had been a calf tethered behind the hut (the Governor and his men, I learnt, had put the rest of it in the fiery stew or 'wat' which they were eating at a discreet distance in another tukal). While I ate, Tafara fussed over the primus preparing coffee, and several times the woman from whom the hut had been commandeered poked her head in the door with shrill cries of delight or protest – Tafara would not disclose which. After a bottle of wine I felt very drowsy, but

PRECEDING PAGES: *Armed to the teeth. From left to right: myself, Teshome, the Governor, Tafara, and twelve barefooted warriors to guard us from shiftas.*

RIGHT: *The journeys to the Mountain, with Jerboa ('a rat with bird's legs'): an illustration in Bruce's* Travels *(1790).*

happy. The flies, which till then had persecuted me without ceasing, seemed to find me less attractive in this condition. They left me, and Tafara too slipped out to look for his own lunch. In the drowsy darkness of the hut, warm and furry like a linen cupboard, I dozed off.

I was woken by a loud halloo. I crept from the hut, blinking in the fierce sunlight, to find the Governor and Teshome taking turns with a pair of field-glasses to observe a small file of men and mules that was threading its way across the chequer-board of fields in the plain below us. Teshome gave a second halloo, and a faint cry, more like an echo than a reply, came back through the thin air. 'They say they're two mules short,' said Teshome, 'but they can catch us up later.' I was rather piqued at the fecklessness of the arrangements, but Teshome assured me that the other mules – only pack-mules he thought – would soon follow. He proved to be correct. Just when the first mule-train was crossing the last millet field at our feet, we saw a second smaller file appear from the direction of the Governor's headquarters at Dagoma. The Governor lowered the pair of field-glasses he carried and complacently announced that now all the preparations were complete.

Soon we were loading up the pack-mules. The munificence of the Governor-General presented the expedition with a considerable problem, though the Governor did his best to shield me from it. The large brown bivouac tent, which had been brought for me, had lost its own collapsible poles and two large steel stakes were to be the substitutes; but no mule could carry these fearsome weapons with any safety. Added to this the packing-case labelled Pernod Fils, in which the canteen, kettle, pots and pans, primus, and further bottles of Moselle had been rudely thrust, was hopelessly top-heavy. I gathered that the Governor suggested that the contents should be distributed evenly on the backs of several mules; or at least the packing-case must be strapped on its side. Tafara, however, would not compromise and insisted it should be upright or the wine would spoil. Tafara carried the day. The three pack-mules – two for my equipment, one for the rest of the party's, sixteen now in number – were accordingly made ready: first a piece of tanned hide about the size of a small groundsheet was laid across their backs to prevent them

from becoming sore; then the load was lowered on to them while two men held their heads and two more their tails to prevent them tossing off their awkward burdens; then somebody would lace a couple of thongs across the load, tightening them with his foot on the mule's side like a lady's maid lacing up stays. In a remarkably short time the mules were loaded. The mules clattered away up the track with the Pernod Fils wobbling madly on one mule, and the two steel tent-poles sticking out from the other like the tusks of an elephant, while a frenzied sound of banging came from inside the Pernod Fils as though someone was crying to be let out. It struck me that in a very short time the mules' packs would be off again.

It was now about mid-afternoon. The shadows cast by the bamboula tree and the conical huts were considerably longer, and the sun less hot than an hour before. After crossing a couple of millet fields the track reached the first foothills of Belesa. The going looked easy enough, though I was far from confident about my powers as a rider. I jammed my topee squarely upon my head, and followed our mule-train as we trotted out after the baggage-mules towards the hills. By now the market had dispersed; the long lines of market-goers had returned across the plain the way they had come.

The first few moments of my career on a mule were both exhausting and perilous: I tried to ride the mule as one would a horse, imposing my will on it, though the Ethiopian bridle which is joined in a loop at the mane would not allow this, and the mule was clearly in no doubt as to who knew best. But after a short time, having no self-respect to lose, I gave up trying and resigned myself to being led by the mule. Apart from the other advantages, I had, as a passenger, far more time to observe the countryside.

First we crossed the millet fields. These were different in one respect from those I had seen close to the motor-road. In the middle of each field, above the thick spears of green corn, rose a platform of eucalyptus boughs built on the supporting trunks of a sort of willow tree, pollarded to a suitable height. On each platform crouched a small boy, so ragged that one might have taken him for a scarecrow if one hadn't seen him move. I asked Teshome if they were in fact there to scare the birds away – I hadn't seen any flocks of

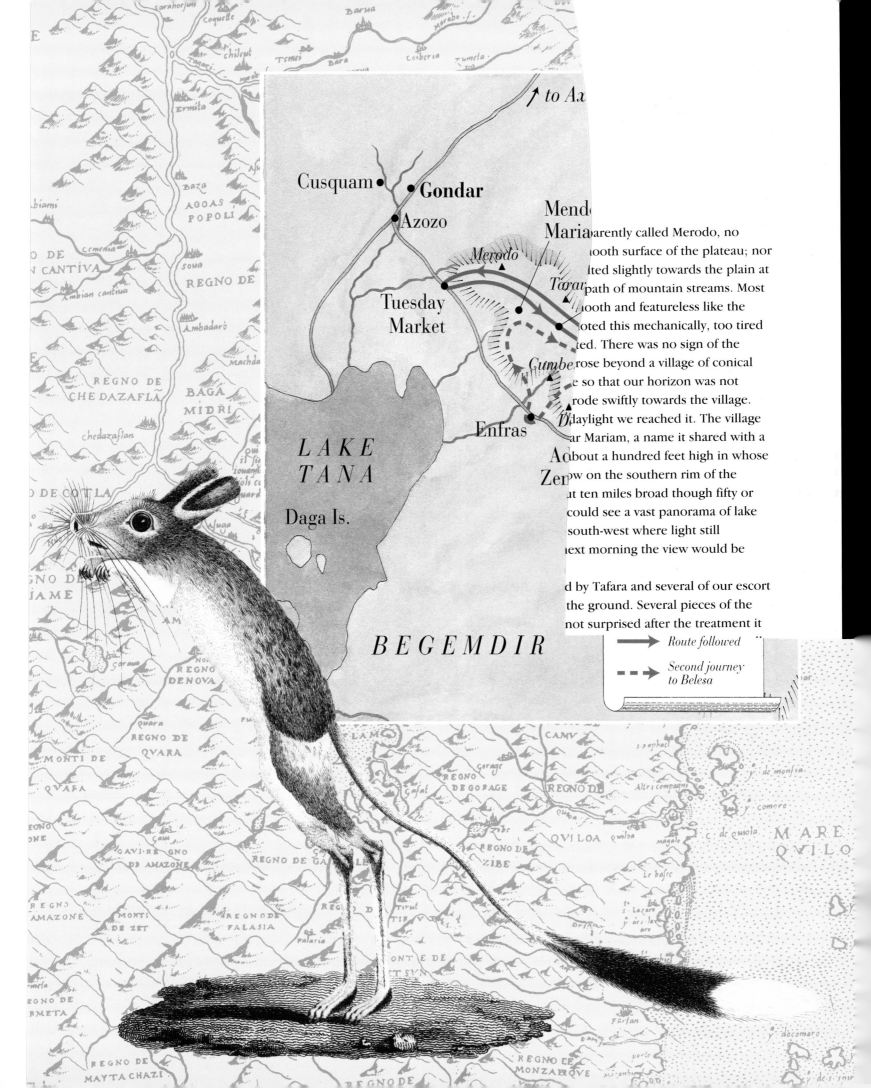

Cusquam • • **Gondar**

• Azozo

Mend○
Maria

Merodo ▲

Tara

Tuesday
Market

Cumbe ▲

▲

Enfras

D

Ad○

Ze○

LAKE
TANA

Daga Is.

BEGEMDIR

...arently called Merodo, no
...ooth surface of the plateau; nor
...lted slightly towards the plain at
...path of mountain streams. Most
...ooth and featureless like the
...oted this mechanically, too tired
...ted. There was no sign of the
...rose beyond a village of conical
...e so that our horizon was not
...rode swiftly towards the village.
...daylight we reached it. The village
...ar Mariam, a name it shared with a
...bout a hundred feet high in whose
...w on the southern rim of the
...t ten miles broad though fifty or
...could see a vast panorama of lake
...south-west where light still
...ext morning the view would be

...d by Tafara and several of our escort
...the ground. Several pieces of the
...not surprised after the treatment it

→ *Route followed*

⇢ *Second journey
to Belesa*

We had to be back at Tuesday Market in three days – a ridiculously tight schedule I thought, but what could I, an ignorant guest, say about it? It was one of the few times that I found an Ethiopian seriously worried by a schedule.

lighter colour of my companions, everybody was huddled in blankets. I shivered in my light gaberdine coat and jodhpurs. The Governor offered me a spare rug. Soon, like an obedient troop around their scoutmaster, we were all sitting cross-legged around him.

'How far are we from Wehni?' I asked when I found a polite opening. 'Oh, almost within sight.' In the highlands, when you can sometimes see a hundred miles, this was not very definite. 'Tomorrow we will show you.' The Governor was tolerant with my impatience to know plans in advance. But clearly he preferred to produce the Mountain for me like a rabbit out of a hat. The conventions of politeness and the difficulties of translation made it impossible for me to ask anyone else how far we were away. I tried my second question. 'Do the men think we shall get up?' The Governor smiled benignly and spoke; Teshome translated: 'He says we will do our best for you. But he says he must admit that all the men say it is impossible. To reach the summit you must climb a rock like this,' he showed his thumb expressively, 'but there is much furniture on top certainly.' 'How do they know if they have never climbed it?' 'We will ask', came the patient reply. But as usual nobody knew.

I slunk away to my tent where Tafara had made up a bed for me, a real bed of sheets and blankets and an air mattress. Tafara smiled wanly. He looked tired himself. 'Tomorrow,' he said, 'Wehni.' Then he left me. I was glad to be alone. There were moments when the peculiar isolation of my position – here I was on a ceremonial progress through the countryside insulated from all problems by my patient and solicitous companions – was distinctly irksome to me. Now I was grateful for the lonely state to which I was

consigned. I felt tired and demoralized. What if the approach to the summit was really the shape of a thumb?

I slept lightly. Once I woke to hear the crackle of dry wood burning and the burr of conversation; later, it seemed hours later, I was woken by Tafara with a piece of roast mutton politely offered me on a plate.

When I next awoke it was dawn, and Tafara was up already preparing breakfast. I peered from the tent flap. It was cold, but the wind had fallen, and the cold had a crispness to it that I found most pleasant. A thousand feet lower than our camp site a veil of mist covered the plain to the west, hiding the spectacular view more completely even than the dark of the evening before. I wandered across to the second tent. The Governor was just strapping on his Sam Browne belt; Teshome was fully dressed. 'We are ready when you have had breakfast.' I asked if they had had theirs already. 'Today is the fast.' I remembered it was Wednesday. Every Wednesday and Friday a good Christian in Ethiopia must fast till midday. This rule applies throughout the year, and in Lent every day is a fast day. Travelling did not apparently give a reason to be excused. I returned rather smugly to my repast – coffee with eggs and slices of roast mutton from the night before. We struck camp and were off before the mist left the plain.

As the light improved I began to take thorough stock of the plateau. The grassy downs ahead of us were not as flat as they had seemed in the dusk. Beyond the ridge, we could now see a range of blue hills that must be quite a thousand feet higher than the plateau. The Governor pointed out the landmarks, taking the opinion, often disputed, of the three local men of our escort; the peaks were apparently called Doumi and Warkamba respectively. There were also five or six humpy volcanic hills close at hand on the sloping rims of the plateau: Tarara, Cumbel, Awara and Chiara, as well as Merodo which stood close to the path we had followed up on to the plateau. Together these grassy hills made the plateau grander than I had thought possible – their pyramidal shapes setting off the horizontal lines of the rolling downs. But where was Wehni? Asfa pointed to the ridge ahead. 'When we are there, we shall be able to see it.' We trotted on past a couple of freshly ploughed fields and an avenue of tall elm-like korch trees, bypassed a village of

The Happy Valley

hardly more than a dozen rude huts, and came to a little brook running a few feet below the springy grassland, clear and deep and straight like an irrigation channel. It must have been six feet wide. The mules took it at a run, and somehow I stayed upright. The pack-mules on the other hand ran amok, and Pernod Fils had to be reloaded. Another ploughed field and we had gained the ridge.

In the many months that I had thought about the Mountain, I had often wondered what shape and size it would be. Would it be a low mound with a mere twenty feet of rock to protect it, or an immense table-mountain whose summit would be a natural fortress? The only evidence was that the Mountain's top must be large enough to hold 200 to 300 princes and their escorts. Both Debra Damo and Amba Geshen rise several hundred feet above the surrounding plain, and their summits are about a mile in circumference. In general I thought Wehni, the third prison-mountain, would be somewhat their shape and size.

From the ridge we had breasted we could see that the plateau rolled on much as before towards the two peaks, Tarara and Cumbel. There were a number of villages directly ahead; one, wealthier than the rest and in a commanding position, was the possessor of a remarkably large church shrouded in a clump of junipers. The plateau itself dipped and was invisible again till it rose like a great breaker in the long ridge of Doumi, Wad and Warkamba. There was no sign of a mountain that could, I thought, be Wehni.

'It is really there?' I asked Teshome anxiously. Apart from the hills whose names I already knew, there was not even a low mound that could have been Wehni.

'We will ask,' said Teshome as patiently as ever. A moment's consultation. 'Yes, there it is, Mr Pakenham. They say that Wehni is there. You can see the top half sticking over the ridge. It is much higher of course. That is just the top.' I still could not see anything which remotely resembled my mental picture of Wehni. Then I saw where Teshome was pointing. A short stump of black rock was just visible above the ridge ten miles away. This was the summit of Wehni. My stomach contracted with fear. It was not the approach to the summit that was the shape of a thumb. The Mountain itself was.

> The place which the wisdom or policy of antiquity had destined for the residence of the Abyssinian princes was a spacious valley in the Kingdom of Amhara, surrounded on every side by mountains... The sides of the mountains were covered with trees, the banks of the brooks were diversified with flowers; every blast shook spices from the rocks, and every month dropped fruits upon the ground.
>
> Johnson: *Rasselas*

I had been conscious for some time that the numbers of our party varied. Once I counted only fifteen in all; at other times we were a formidable procession of nearly thirty men, nearly half of whom were mounted. The explanation for this was a curious one. When our escort of barefooted soldiers became bored with walking or their feet were cut by the outcrops of flint, they commandeered any horse or mule they saw close to our route; this was not difficult as the fertile plateau was dotted with mules and horses. The wretched owners who saw these acts of piracy were thus forced to follow our procession in order to recover their beasts, and our numbers swelled accordingly.

The plateau which we had followed for some twenty miles was now reaching a second climacteric. The ridge ahead of us rose in folds of grassy brown earth; Wehni was temporarily out of sight and only the top of the great Doumi range was visible beyond the ridge. With increasing excitement I rode after the Governor along the pitted track. A tatterdemalion band of armed men passed us, bowing from the waist to the Governor, and rather nonplussed by the sight of me. They were followed by two more men with rifles, and a third whose revolver and white topee marked him as being some sort of local chief. He shook hands and talked respectfully for a moment to the Governor, then joined on to the procession. He was apparently the local governor of this part of Belesa, the Governor's direct subordinate. He hazarded a friendly greeting for me, as he took one of the soldier's mules surrendered to him by merit of his rank.

The Governor of Belesa and the Mountain. The staircase cut in the rock is visible a mile away.

From the crest of the ridge the last half of the plateau was finally revealed. The vast natural forces which had thrown up these smooth regular downs had suddenly run wild. In the docile plain there opened a gorge perhaps half a mile wide, leading to a bowl-shaped valley. It was the valley of Wehni. From the centre rose the scoriated black thumb that was the Mountain. It was in fact twice the height it had first appeared, its sides perfectly sheer to the ground, its top flat and grassy. Once again my stomach contracted with fear.

To the east of this valley the ground climbed steadily to the dorsal ridge of Wad and Doumi, while to the south it was protected by a saddle of ground running more or less level from our plateau to the far range of hills. To the north the ground fell sharply in a long gully to the plain below. These violent changes in terrain were clearly the work of erosion. As in a geological diagram one could see how, over a long period, water, pressing hard on the tableland at this point, had made a basin in the plateau, which drained the rain from three sides down the long gully into the lowlands several thousand feet below. Why had the tableland been weakest at this part? The geological explanation was this: the Wehni valley had once been the base of a volcano whose tufaceous rock had been softer than its surroundings, while the basaltic core of the volcano had been hard enough to survive. The Mountain was all that remained of an immense volcano.

Even the party were moved by the spectacular scenery. The Governor indicated that I might take his photograph if I wanted. Before we moved on I posed him against a fairy backdrop of shimmering wild olives and atwat trees that crowded the luxuriantly green valley. After the dry grass of the downs and the sparsely scattered wild olives of the korch and atwat trees that had dotted the plateau, the valley was indeed amazingly fertile. The path down through the gorge led between tall hedges of evergreens among which I recognized many species of European flowers and shrubs, as well as some entirely new to me – wild roses, for instance, their white petals hanging in clusters, a few yellow roses past their prime, a tangle of plants with the thick leaves and strong smell of sage, strange plants whose leaves and flowers reminded me of Victorian wool flowers under a glass dome, and many fine examples of flowering aloes. It was exactly the right exotic scenery for the Happy Valley of Rasselas.

I was just thinking of Johnson's idyllic description when we came to a brook pouring across the path which for some reason terrified the mule-train; perhaps from the level of a mule's eye it appeared deeper than it was. At any rate each mule shied violently when it came to the brook, and the more temperamental pair were quite unmanageable. Somehow I coaxed my terrified animal to cross the brook, hardly six feet of shallow running water, and followed the

I still could not see anything which remotely resembled my mental picture of Wehni. Then I saw where Teshome was pointing. A short stump of black rock was just visible above the ridge ten miles away. This was the summit of Wehni. My stomach contracted with fear. It was not the approach to the summit that was the shape of a thumb. The Mountain itself was.

Governor up the path beyond. Tafara and Teshome were not so fortunate. Teshome's mule leaped from the path to avoid the waters of the evil brook, and had dashed its rider against the thorny bough of an acacia bush before regaining the path; Tafara's mule tried to leap the brook itself, though the path was as usual littered with large stones which had rolled from the bank above. The mule's feet skidded as it landed, and in recovering itself it threw Tafara headlong on to the path. He was luckily only shaken and soon remounted. It was the first time I saw a mule make a serious mistake, and I should have taken more notice of the circumstances. Later on I was to regret this keenly, but for the moment we congratulated each other on our escapes and trotted on past similar brooks, which incomprehensibly presented no fears to our mounts, while the Mountain loomed ahead, growing larger and at the same time squatter in shape as the path left the gorge and circled round to approach the village of Wehni from the south.

It was now late in the afternoon. With the slanting sun at our backs we forded two streams of clear, cold mountain water, and passed the groves of willow-like dokama trees that grew along their banks. Once we heard a bird singing near by with the strong, double call of a shepherd's pan-pipe. It was called a 'gurramailee', Teshome said, and had brilliant plumage, but we never caught sight of it; the exotic bird flew off, keeping to the trees as a cuckoo will, and calling in its strong, musical voice as it flew.

Wehni itself hardly deserved the name of a village. It was a rough circle of huts built on a grassy mound in the bowl-shaped valley. Some of the huts were uninhabited, others no more than cattle byres. There was no local governor or anyone to salute the Governor with authority; the inhabitants looked wretchedly poor and ill, especially one with a swollen face who asked pitifully if the Frank was a doctor. The rest greeted us with sullen stares. It was easy to guess what they were thinking. They could ill afford to entertain so large a party as ours.

For the moment we left them to their forebodings and trotted on past the village to the church ahead. The Governor was eager to make contact with the priests, I to see if there were frescoes or manuscripts of an early date in the church. We dismounted and walked down to the knoll where the church lay hidden in its cloak of junipers.

The towering juniper trees around it were certainly good evidence that it might be of early date; the junipers on the highlands take some two hundred years to grow to their full height. We crossed a field bright with scarlet thistles, and came to the church wall. It was not as high or as grand as Michael Debra's, but the stones of the wall were clearly of some antiquity; the mud cement had been washed away from between the outside stones leaving them precariously balanced. Inside the church was very ramshackle. The conical roof of brown thatch bound at the top into a miniature spire of straw was hopelessly lop-sided, while the bamboo stockade, which in poor churches is all there is to protect the outer ambulatory, was ruinous. We peered through the stockade to see if anyone was inside, but the inside doors of the church were firmly locked and all the shutters barred.

The priests, whose hut was near by, slipped noiselessly into the churchyard soon after we had arrived. Like most country priests only their white turbans distinguished them from village elders; they were barefooted, both carried fly-whisks and wore baggy trousers; and white shammas hung in folds over their shirts, as seemed usual for countrymen of means. They greeted the Governor politely, the older priest holding out a silver cross for him to kiss.

After a moment the Governor turned to me. Teshome

THE HAPPY VALLEY

translated: 'They say the church was built by Fasil, and there are many pictures; they invite you to enter.' I refused to allow my hopes to be raised too much, but I gladly took off my shoes and padded after them into the dusty interior. The floor of the outer ambulatory was of baked earth, and our footfalls were muffled by its cool marble-like surface. We waited, as one would wait for some mystical rite to begin, for the inner doorway to be unlocked. The elder of the two priests unhooked from his pocket a curiously shaped key – it was almost like a sort of boat-hook – and inserted it into a rough hole in the wooden doorway. Eventually the bolt behind was pushed back, and the door creaked open. A dusty aroma, as of long-matured pot-pourri, rolled out – the floor was knee-deep in hay. We followed the priests into the inner chamber. As the light improved I saw the walls of the rectangular sanctuary were richly decorated with paintings.

After the first flush of excitement I made a careful analysis of their subjects. There was a most striking St George on the left of the sanctuary doorway, a fine Madonna to the right, and the usual gory martyrdoms dear to Ethiopia. The paintings probably dated from the late seventeenth century, fifty years after Fasil in fact, but were exciting evidence of the importance of Wehni at that time. Though the church and village were now so dilapidated, it was obvious that once they had enjoyed royal patronage as munificent as Gondar itself. The paintings were in as fine a hand as those of the church of Debra Berhan Selassie at Gondar. I took a number of photographs to record the paintings, though the light was very dim, necessitating a time-exposure of more than a minute for the colour film. With this valuable evidence tucked in my camera, we withdrew from the church, and after thanking the priests, took our leave. The Mountain, invisible behind the ring of junipers, lay directly ahead. The priests followed, whether from historical interest or mere curiosity, their grave mien did not betray.

It was an hour before sunset. The declining rays of the sun were directly behind us as we stepped out of the church's juniper grove, lighting up the scene with a yellow theatrical glare. The valley lay at our feet, a cascade of trees and flowering shrubs. Out of it rose the vast, craggy bulk of the Mountain. Our position on the very last platform of the plateau was an admirable vantage-point to observe it from,

St George and the Dragon. A seventeenth-century fresco I discovered in the church below the Mountain.

for the ground fell so sharply that its base, hardly a quarter of a mile away, was considerably lower than we, and we were level with a point a third of the way up its flanks. While the Governor and his escort sank down under some trees like wild chestnuts (apparently they were called gotom trees), I borrowed field-glasses, and studied every detail. The priests withdrew to a discreet distance and watched us attentively.

I didn't need field-glasses to see the first point. The cleft up the north face was, just as I had guessed, a man-made path hewn from the sheer walls of the rock. Facilidas' masons must have cut this path up the north side of the amba as the rock face there was the least vertical, though much longer than the south face immediately opposite us. I wondered what hope it offered us to climb. Time would show whether the steps which must surely have been cut in the rock were still preserved. Without some form of help our prospects looked bleak indeed, for though the north face was least steep at the end, the first few hundred feet was perfectly sheer like the other sides. In all we would have three or four

hundred feet to climb; while on the farther side the amba must be more than six hundred feet high.

About the scale I was, and still am, very puzzled. The amba seemed, as we stood on our grassy platform facing it across the chasm, about three or four hundred feet high; this one judged by the relative size of the trees around us, and on the grassy summit opposite. But as we were looking at the least tall side this would make the amba average nearer six hundred feet. From the photographs taken farther off which included both the juniper trees and the church, about sixty feet high, one reaches the same conclusion. But I cannot even now say with any accuracy how high Wehni is. I much regret not having taken instruments to measure its height.

The second point was equally exciting; we could clearly discern buildings on the Mountain. Through the Governor's field-glasses I saw a semicircular wall at the foot of the north face where the steps presumably began. At a point on the path about three-quarters of the way up was a small honey-coloured fort, apparently well preserved. It was built in the

South Arabian style of some Gondarin buildings – differing from the forts of South Arabia only in the materials used – with two arrow slits in the blank wall and four corner pinnacles. Above the fort the path zigzagged up to the summit. Here, packed together on a site no larger than two grass tennis-courts, was a small colony of ruined buildings – a tower with a lancet window and a walled approach like the gate-house to Facilidas' castle at Gondar; a roofless, gabled church of the same shape as at Debra Berhan, with round-headed windows and charred rafters clearly visible; and all about lines of horizontal stone walls showing through the high grass. Despite the grass and the trees that cluttered the small free space on the summit, this was proof enough, if proof was needed, that there had once been a sizeable settlement on this stalagmite of rock. Now its only inhabitants were a colony of brown kites that circled the amba ceaselessly, the black rocks flecked with white from their droppings like the gannet-haunted Skelligs off the Kerry coast.

It would remain to be seen if we could climb the path and discover more about the life that was lived there. The priests, sitting gravely under the gotom trees, did not for the moment hazard an opinion. They were content to observe me in silence. I asked if any of the men thought we should be able to climb up. The Governor was mute too. On this rather forbidding note we returned to the tents which had been set up in our absence. A ragged group of village children, whose parents must have provided a sheep for our evening meal, sat watching hungrily as we ate. My appetite was not good that evening and their patience was soon rewarded.

I slept little that night. After a hurried meat breakfast I began to dress for the ordeal of the ascent.

There is a note in the 1860 edition of Murray's *Guide to Egypt* which reads: 'If the traveller inquires whether the oriental dress be necessary, I answer it is by no means so; and a person wearing it, who is ignorant of the language, becomes ridiculous. One remark, however, I must be allowed to make on dress in the East – that a person is never respected who is badly dressed, of whatever kind the costume may be, and nowhere is exterior appearance so much thought of as in the East.'

These severe words, which I took to apply to rural Ethiopia today as well as they had to the Egypt of the Khedivate, were indeed food for thought. I realized that my golf jacket, khaki trousers and third-rate topee were not impressive as a costume. At this crisis in my affairs I needed every assistance I could get. But my smart clothes were aggressively Ethiopian. I had bought an outfit of Ethiopian dress – baggy white trousers called Tafari-cut after the Emperor, and long Arab-style smock here called a jitterbub – in an Armenian tailor's in Addis Ababa, more for their merits as fancy dress when I returned, than for their practical use on the expedition. I wondered if I should appear ridiculous if I wore them now, speaking hardly a word of the language as I did. I glanced at Teshome and the Governor. In their eyes I was clearly a figure of fun already; nothing then could be lost by wearing it before them. But to the unsophisticated majority – the villagers, and the priests and the hungry small boys – these handsome traditional garments might appear most impressive. At any rate I enjoyed the absurdity of wearing them. I struggled into the white robes, tied camera, compass and Coptic cross around my neck (there were naturally no pockets) and followed the Governor and Teshome down the pebbly hill towards the church. They were led by a young man from a village with the frizzy locks and goat-like appearance of a satyr.

Where the path forked, one path going up to the church and the other continuing down the valley, the two priests sat awaiting us. A cool wind blew through the silver leaves of olives shading the path. The priests greeted us gravely; as before, the Governor went forward and kissed the proffered silver cross, and the rest followed suit. In my white robes I felt bold enough to hazard a kiss too. The elder priest held the cross up to my lips and I touched the four corners as ritual demanded. The priest replaced the cross in its red calico handkerchief, and began to address the Governor. From time to time the Governor nodded in assent.

The priests, it appeared, were warning us of the dangers of trying to climb the amba. Their mood of quietism had changed. As the chief representatives of the village they felt it their duty to warn us. 'What did you say?' I asked the Governor rather peevishly. 'Did you agree with them?' The Governor did not reply. We left the two Cassandras under the olive trees.

As the path became steeper, the flowers and shrubs

BELOW: *I put
on my jitterbub to
dazzle the locals.*

became more luxuriant. The auburn gotom trees of the evening before were thicker here than ever, and at their feet grew white woolly flowers with yellow petals called 'injaurtz'; there was also a new species, a gina tree, whose thin silver leaves reminded me of an olive, though its trunk was smoother and darker. We had to cut our way past these exotic obstacles, and our hands and legs became flecked with tiny burrs. I was glad of the generous protection of my jitterbub.

After ten minutes, where the defile ran between two craggy rocks, I was excited to see a long wall with grass-choked arrow-slits piercing its sides in several places. The yellow stones were fixed together with lime cement. These were clearly the ruins of a fort built by the Kings of Gondar – even such elementary architecture as this was unknown beyond their sphere of influence – and still more evidence of the importance of the Mountain. Here a check point had been constructed to guard the last mile of the road. Perhaps it was here that one of the few prisoners ever to escape, the future King Hannes, had been recaptured by the palace guards.

Beyond the fort the path became more precipitous still as it approached the foot of the amba. We could hardly keep pace with out goat-like guide. He leapt from boulder to boulder with the assurance of long practice, but we were less adroit; twice I slipped and was forced to grasp the spiky leaves of acacia for support. Eventually, perhaps after ten minutes of this slithering descent, we came to a circular wall cemented to the foot of the amba. Its stones closely resembled the fort's in shape and colour. Owing to the thick mat of undergrowth it was difficult to see at first that both ends of the wall were attached to the actual rock of the amba. But this was in fact the case. The great wall must have been used to enclose the open space where the King and his Court camped when they paid a visit to the Governor of the Mountain. I thought of the scene which must have been enacted here – Bruce describes it at length – when King Yasous set up his camp here and ordered all the prisoners to be brought down from the Mountain. Nowadays the courtyard is choked with tall grass and young saplings. We waded though the grass and stood surveying the amba.

The rock path began in a series of steps cut from the volcanic rock like the steps at Petra that lead to the temple called Ed Deir. We could follow the rust-coloured scar for some thirty feet above our heads, until it reached a place where the rock was overhanging; at this point a second fort had been built, cemented on to the rock face like a house-martin's nest. Whether the steps continued beyond was impossible to see.

The moment had arrived for the ascent. The party quickly divided itself into those who felt honour demanded some attempt at climbing, and those who were content to stand below and encourage (or deride) our efforts; the first category comprised only the Governor, Teshome and two of the soldiers who had been most importunate in their demands to be photographed, the brashest of our escort in fact; all the rest, including the local governor with the identical marque of topee as my own, withdrew to a safe distance.

ABOVE: *Teshome and the Governor inspect the route up the Mountain from below.*

Summit of the Mountain covered in ruins.
The second fort is visible on the rock path
just to the left of the central shadow. The
third fort and wall guard the summit.

First Teshome, a gallant figure in his wide-awake, started up the staircase. The Governor removed his Sam Browne and topee and followed. I clambered after them. It was easy going up to the fort, as a thick succulent called 'andahula' which grew in the crevices between the stairs, provided an excellent handhold. The three of us, installed in the dank interior of the roofless fort, peered upwards at the rock face. Thirty feet of overhanging rock towered above. There were no traces of any steps, but over to the right where it seemed the staircase must have been run, the rock was flaked and pitted by a recent landslide.

For several minutes we sat there without speaking. Asfa and Teshome were, I suppose, relieved that our ascent was cut short with such finality. I was wrapped in a numbing mist of disappointment. 'It is no good,' said the Governor at length. 'Perhaps later we can bring ropes and a long ladder to climb the rock. But let us go down now.' My companions left me.

Suddenly I had a wild idea that I could crawl round beyond the area of the landslide. I crawled along a narrowing ledge till I was firmly and ignominiously wedged. Looking down I could see the men of the escort grinning; this was their chance. I wondered humbly what would happen to me. With remarkable agility, the goat-like man who had led us came flying up the rock face towards me. When he was five feet away he took a sickle-shaped knife, that rested in his frizzy hair like a pencil over an errand-boy's ear, and stretched its handle to me. I seized it gratefully. Soon I was restored to the ground.

The two priests who had prophesied disaster had followed us. They were talking complacently to the Governor when I came up. They had good reason to be smug, I reflected. But how much did they know, I wondered, about the landslide? I asked Teshome to see if anyone they knew had climbed the amba before the path disappeared. They replied that years ago, perhaps thirty years ago, a priest called Skinder Mariam had climbed the staircase to the summit. I asked what he had found. 'Oh,' they replied, 'he had found a curiously shaped vase.' 'Where is it now?' 'Oh, it broke – and naturally we threw away the pieces.'

This assertion started a furious controversy among the villagers who had followed the priests down to a courtyard. There was said to be an old man in the village still alive who had actually climbed the Mountain. It was he, not Skinder Mariam, who had climbed to the top. 'Wait,' said the goat-like man, 'he is my father. I will call him. He is near by.' He gave a loud cry which floated across the valley, echoing off the walls of the amba to the alarm of the kites above. Soon an old man, very tall for an Amhara, in a particularly dirty grey shamma, stumbled down the path towards us. Both sides waited eagerly. Teshome put the question to him. 'Yes,' he replied, 'it was I who climbed with five others from the village. We thought there might be treasure on top. There were wooden steps at that time. When we reached the tower a little distance from the summit, we were afraid to go on.' 'What were you afraid of?' I interrupted. 'They say that devils have lived there since the King's sons left in the reign of King Tekla Georghis. But one of our number was braver and climbed to the summit.' 'Did he find any treasure?' 'No, but

LEFT: *Before the ascent we passed a ruined checkpoint.*
BELOW: *At the foot of the Mountain.*
RIGHT: *Where I got stuck.*

For several minutes
we sat there without
speaking. Asfa and
Teshome were, I
suppose, relieved that
our ascent was cut
short with such
finality. I was wrapped
in a numbing mist of
disappointment.

there were remains of many stone houses – enough for the
King's sons who numbered more than two hundred. And in
the middle there was a great house.' I tried to discover more,
but he would only repeat what he had said. 'The wooden
steps fell in the ruins many years ago. You cannot climb
now.' He turned away. 'He will not let his son try,' said the
soldiers grinning. 'No one can climb the amba now.'

That afternoon I rode gloomily out of the valley, with
many a backward glance at the Mountain. I wondered how I
could arrange to return and climb to the 'great house'. The
identification of the site of the Mountain, more melodramatic
than even Bruce's account suggested; the discovery of guard
posts and check-points in the style of the Gondar palaces; a
glimpse from below of the summit itself still bearing traces of
the prison-town built there; details of the Mountain which
were all confirmed by surviving local traditions – this was no
compensation for the failure to reach the summit. I rode
back across the plateau more or less insensible to what we
passed, so heavily did our failure weigh down on me.

We camped in a large village on the western tip of the
plateau whose name was unknown to me. I was too
dispirited to care. The soldiers built a fire and roasted a
sheep whole, drinking 'talla' far into the night. I slept poorly.
Next morning we left before the mist rose from the plains.

Chapter Three

The Feast of the Epiphany

ABOVE: *The canyon of the Blue Nile where we picnicked and I mistook my companions for baboons.* RIGHT: *The Blue Nile Falls.* PRECEDING: *Sailing on Lake Tana, and* (RIGHT), *a priest in a reed canoe or tankwa.*

No sooner had the crosses first touched the pool than two or three hundred boys, calling themselves deacons, plunged in with only a white cloth or rag tied around their middle ... Everybody else went close down to the edge of the pool where water was thrown upon them, and first decently enough; but after the better sort of person had received the aspersion the whole was turned into a riot, the boys, muddying the water, threw it around upon everyone they saw well-dressed or clean.

Bruce's description of Timkat at Gondar

Back at the guest-house I turned with a renewed sense of urgency to planning a second expedition to the Mountain. Two things I had lacked – proper climbing equipment and a proper knowledge about climbing. In the next day or two I tried various members of the European colony to see if I could borrow equipment and enlist the services of a mountaineer. Much the most helpful was Dr Jäger.

Dr Jäger was a mild-eyed, most civilized man in his late fifties. He and his wife both worked for W.H.O. which had sent them first to Teheran, then to Baghdad, now at length to Gondar. I took to them both at once. 'Of course you must climb up,' said Frau Jäger when she had heard my story. 'Otto might come with you, though he is too old for climbing. We have a friend, a German engineer who lives down on Lake Tana. He is a very keen mountaineer. I am sure he would be best able to help you.'

It was arranged that the following weekend we should go to Lake Tana. I could join them in an excursion and later we might be able to interest Herr Deinigger, the engineer at Gorgora, in my plans for the second Wehni expedition.

The excursion itself was entirely delightful. The two actual objects of our expedition – a bridge built by King Facilidas across the Blue Nile and the mummified body of the King on the island of Daga – were both equally elusive, but we were not at all cast down at missing them; it was more than enough to sail across the blue surface of the lake in a tankwa, an undulating reed canoe, to picnic in the canyon where the Nile began its long downhill course to the Mediterranean, to enjoy the thunder of the Falls and to sleep in the intriguing little village of Bahr Dahr, destined according to one plan to be the future capital of Ethiopia. Today Bahr Dahr gives no hint of future greatness; it is so poor that we could not even buy a round of bread. [1998: It is now an admirable holiday resort.]

One incident I remember vividly occurred during the abortive search for the bridge. I was some way from the rest of the party, and in the high African grass I soon lost my sense of direction. Rather self-consciously I began to shout to attract my party's attention. My halloos echoed across the dense woods of sycamore and fig tree; a pair of toucans flapped off at the noise. Then I saw, along a liana-hung path

in the wood, a line of people approaching. 'Dr Jäger,' I cried, 'I *am* glad to see you.' The line of people halted, peering at me quizzically through the undergrowth. It was a family of baboons. We both retreated hastily. Shortly afterwards I found the party where I had left them, not yet having missed me. The story of identity mistaken, though it has since served me well, did not go down best with the Jägers.

Before we returned to Gondar I had persuaded Herr Deinigger to accompany me on the second expedition to Wehni. The Epiphany holiday, ten days hence, would suit him best, as he would then be free to leave Gorgora for the weekend. The problems of mountaineering equipment he felt well able to solve. There must be a rope in Gondar or if necessary one could be flown from Addis; while the 'pitons' or iron spikes for the overhanging sections of the rock face

were easily made in the machine shop at Gorgora. With high hopes I returned to the ghibbi guest-house.

I had not, however, reckoned with the peculiarities of Herr Deinigger's contract to work in Ethiopia; he was apparently forbidden to leave Gorgora without permission; this permission was withdrawn on the day before he was due to join me in Gondar, apparently because of the supposed dangers of trying to climb the Mountain. Hope languished. I decided to fly back to Addis the day after the Epiphany. I would have to reorganize my plans in the capital.

I had a particular reason for staying at Gondar for the Feast of the Epiphany, or Timkat, which is exceptional in that the main ceremonial takes place away from the church by a river or pool of water. In Addis Ababa this adds no particular interest to the ceremony, as the procession repairs from the charmlessness of modern stone churches, to a characterless concrete pool by the imperial polo ground. Gondar, on the other hand, is an ideal place to attend Timkat celebrations. The chief churches of Gondar send a procession of priests and parishioners out of the city down to the green valley of the Caa. Here in the grounds of the summer palace, haunted by egrets and sacred ibis, is the bathing-pool that has been used for Timkat since the time of King Facilidas. The ceremonies themselves last three days in all: on Timkat eve the procession converges on the pool; the priests spend the night encamped by it in company with the Arks taken from each church; they return in procession after the ceremonies next morning; on the following day, the Feast of Michael, there is a second procession within the town walls, and a strange equestrian game called Guks is traditionally played.

This was the general picture I got from the reports – some of them conflicting – current in Gondar during the week I waited for Herr Deinigger. I watched with interest tinged with disappointment – at that time I thought I should be off on my second trip to the Mountain – the preparations for the ceremony. The bathing-pool, which was normally dry at this season, had to be filled from the river Caa by the culvert built for this purpose by King Facilidas; last year it had been patched up and was now working again. Day by day the pool filled up; by Wednesday it was spilling over into the grassy courtyard. On Thursday when I found that the expedition would have to be indefinitely postponed, I

realized that as a minor compensation I could now attend Timkat where it is best seen in all Ethiopia.

It was a quarter to seven on the morning of Timkat, and the sun had not yet risen from behind the long tree-spattered ridge where Gondar lay spread out above us. Under the juniper trees in the courtyard of the summer palace it was chilly. A crowd of ragged children had lit small bonfires of leaves to warm themselves by. The main crowd was huddled against the north wall of the courtyard, wrapped in their white woollen shammas like the pupae of moths wrapped in their cocoons. I wandered across to the north wall; at one end was a row of stables. Here the priests from the seven churches of Gondar had camped for the night, holding converse with the seven Arks of the Covenant. The crowd pressed closely round the entrance. From inside came the dull boom of kettle-drums, the muffled chant of priests singing, the chink of bells and rattles, and the plaintive cries of babies; with the sound an exotic odour compounded of incense and crushed eucalyptus leaves and sweat rolled out on the frosty air. Tibet, I thought, must offer scenes like this.

Two hours later the atmosphere changed completely. A strong yellow sun tessellated the stucco walls of the summer palace, picking out the round-headed battlements and the tall windows looking on to the pool. Below, a pullulating mass of spectators pressed round the pool, threatening to send those at the front into the water. At their left stood the Bishop and the priests of the seven churches; their seven Arks were concealed by wrappings of gorgeous brocades and canopied by ceremonial umbrellas. The crowd hushed as the Bishop, dressed in black and wearing a cylindrical hat like those worn by Orthodox priests in Greece, took a gold cross affixed to a long staff and dipped it in the water three times. He then took a little water in his cupped hands and blessed the congregation, sprinkling them with it. These rites were curiously familiar to a Catholic – not at all as I had expected.

But a new spirit now seized the ceremonies. After the Abuna, the priests near by took water in more generous quantities and blessed the congregation. The congregation then began to bless each other. Soon there was a regular water fight. A dozen or so children had jumped fully clothed into the pool and were swimming frantically about in the green water; their ecstatic cries and splashes drove some of

the spectators to shelter under a fig tree growing by one of the enclosure walls. Here they were a sitting target for a party of fanatical small boys. I saw several eminent members of the foreign community doused with the holy water at point-blank range; Colonel Tamarat, too, was under fire for a short time until a brave posse of policemen formed a protective cordon round him. It was clearly an excellent opportunity to work off old scores; Timkat appeared to give complete immunity to the small boys. This is in the grand Ethiopian tradition. Christmas, too, gives immunity of this sort and in the old days, according to Bruce, the Christmas festivities were not complete unless the game of 'ganna' (a sort of hockey) had resulted in the death of several players.

The orgy of splashing finally ended, but not before the level of the pool was noticeably lower and the limestone walls of the enclosure several shades darker in colour. The priests of the seven churches now formed up in the courtyard around the pool. First in the procession were the boy deacons, dressed in copes the colour of amethyst, emerald and gold; each church might provide three or four to carry missals and candles. Behind them were the priests themselves, with the chief priest carrying the Ark of the church on his head, itself invisible under a rich pall of gold and purple brocade. Then came the 'debtera' or choirmen, who danced the Dance of David as the procession slowly advanced up the valley back to Gondar.

It is called the Dance of David by travellers, as it is traditionally supposed to be the dance that David danced

before the Ark of the Covenant. The seven processions slowly advanced, gradually fanning out as they headed in the direction of their own churches. At intervals the debtera performed their own strange limping dance. This began very slowly. The two lines of dancers, each holding prayer stick and rattle, swayed to and fro to the beat of a kettle-drummer standing between; as they shuffled forward they sang a slow chant, their tinkling rattles sounded in harmony. Gradually the tempo increased. The two lines advanced and receded in concertina motion, while the kettle-drummer beat an ever fiercer tattoo, till the dance ended on a flurry of drums and rattles and a high-pitched lililil from the crowd. After a pause a bugle sounded and the procession moved on again, and soon the dance was repeated.

By the time the sun was high the long files of priests and worshippers had wound back across the valley towards Gondar, leaving the pool and the summer palace deserted once again. With a rustling noise the sacred ibis, that had been disturbed by the noise of the celebrations, flighted in, settling in the mossy boughs of the junipers. I sat below in what shade was afforded by the honey-coloured walls of the enclosure, and watched the seven processions fade in the distance. The procession from the Church of Caa Jesus had the shortest way to return and its dancers lingered longest in the valley. Just before they had disappeared they passed a long line of humpy cattle filing down to the river to drink. In the contrast between cows and worshippers I found something unexpectedly ludicrous: I laughed aloud. It was

The dance that David danced before the Ark. Inadvertently, I stopped the procession.

LEFT: The summer palace of King Facilidas at Gondar, high and dry after the orgy of splashing was over.

the right moment for a *détente* in a morning that had become unbearably lyrical.

I was flying to Addis on the midday plane next day, the Feast of Michael. After the last of Tafara's meat breakfasts I made my farewells with the European colony. From two I had a particularly warm reception; Dr Jäger promised to be free to accompany me to Wehni the following month, while a charming Anglo-Indian schoolmaster, called Mr Rams, whom I had met once or twice with the Jägers, told me I would be most welcome as his guest when I returned to Gondar.

It remained only to say good-bye to Colonel Tamarat who had sustained with such patience the unenviable job of looking after me during the last month. The Michael procession was still circling the streets of Gondar, and I guessed he would be among the city's dignitaries at its head. I took my bag and followed it. The procession moved quite slowly and I gradually overhauled it, passing first a ragged crowd of townspeople, some carrying flags and banners and

even calendars with the Emperor's portrait loyally held high; occasionally little groups of these did a short dance, egged on by a sort of cheer-leader and emitting the shrill trilling which never failed to thrill me. Nearer the front were the petty officials in their smart Sunday clothes – blue suits, gaberdine trousers and sober-coloured ties; many of their faces were familiar. I noticed my old enemy at the post office ('You are called Mr Thomas; this letter is for Mr Pakenham'), my ally at the Ethiopian Airline office, and various myrmidons of Colonel Tamarat. Close by I found the Governor and Teshome, the companions of my expedition to Wehni; we waved at each other. At last I found Colonel Tamarat. I stepped between the ranks to say good-bye – and for a minute the whole procession halted. We shook hands quickly. 'Good-bye,' he said, 'come back soon.' The procession rolled on again to the Church of Michael.

Three hours later, after crossing in a great bound Lake Tana, Gojjam and the Blue Nile, I was once more in Addis.

The Ascent of Debra Damo

The King of Zeila came against it (the Mountain of Debra Damo) with all his power for a year, but could never capture it; and this was not out of desire for the treasures in it ... but to get the Queen in his hands, whom he much desired, for she is very beautiful ... The manner of the fortification of the Mountain of Debra Damo is in this wise. There is no way up save one narrow path, with a badly made winding stair. Above this is a gate where the guards are, and this gate is ten or twelve fathoms above the point where the path stops, and no one can ascend or descend the hill save by a basket...

Castonhoso, Portuguese
Expedition to Abyssinia in 1541–3

The second Wehni expedition was now maturing as well as could be expected. I had borrowed a climbing rope from a gym mistress at the British Embassy; Dr Jäger wrote to me to confirm that he would be ready to leave in a month; Asserate Kassa said he would be leaving any day for Gondar himself and would organize everything in advance.

While waiting to return to Wehni, I decided to make the journey to Debra Damo. This was crucial to my quest because it was the first prison-mountain of the series. At some time in the early Middle Ages the Kings of Ethiopia chose this Mountain, already famous as the site of a church and monastery founded by Abuna Aragavi, to be the prison guarding the King's relations. Debra Damo ceased to be a prison-mountain after a usurping Queen, named Yudit, surprised the Mountain and put all the princes – some 400 in number – to the sword. But it remained a famous religious centre. It survived the Moslem wars, despite frequent assaults by Mahomet Gran and his Turkish auxiliaries, as no one could scale the rock walls which rose sheer from the ground to its grassy summit; at the worst period of these wars the King himself took refuge there. Later it was to be a refuge for an English missionary, Samuel Gobat (the future first

Anglican Bishop of Jerusalem) who fled there from the marauding Gallas of the area in 1820. To the present day, as I now heard, the monks kept their mountain fortress intact with no little fanaticism .

A few days later I found myself at Makalle, the capital of the northern province of Tigre. I was accompanied by a school friend who worked for a tobacco firm. He was keen to climb to the monastery, and had the essential ingredients for the swift success of the expedition – a car and an interpreter. Debra Damo was still nearly a hundred miles north of us, but I had learned in Addis that it was essential that I should get a letter authorizing me to visit the monastery from the Governor-General of Tigre, Ras Seyum. To him I had a letter of introduction written by Amaha.

I was grateful to have an excuse to visit Ras Seyum. Like Ras Kassa he was one of the few surviving relics of the old feudal nobility; unlike Ras Kassa his record of loyalty to the Emperor was far from unblemished. His claim to the throne was a good one – he was a natural grandson of the Emperor John – and with this claim and his powerful backing in Tigre he was a threat to the power of Ras Tafari throughout the years of his Regency. In 1930, just before Ras Tafari became Emperor, he came out in revolt against the Regent, and one of his sons was killed in battle; though he fought against the Italians in 1935, the Emperor considered him dangerous enough on his return to keep him under surveillance in Addis Ababa; indeed the Emperor's suspicions were borne out when there was a revolt in Tigre in 1943 in which one of his sons is said to have been implicated; afterwards emasculated by the centralization of post-war years, he was allowed to return as Governor-General of Tigre, where he lived, it was said, the life of an invalid and a recluse.

Makalle is a town of stony streets and rough stone houses, a bleak town in a bleak landscape. I was disturbed by the atmosphere. This was a different world from the green plains of the Shoan highlands, and the well-wooded hills around Gondar. And there was a sense of desolation in the city that distressed one. Many of the buildings were in ruins; and there were no new buildings to compensate as there had been at Gondar. I asked an old man in a bar why there was so much damage. He said that I should know; it was we who

canary-yellow cape, and a black pill-box hat, appeared on the path above our heads. 'Who are the Franks?' he demanded fiercely of our interpreter. Two Englishmen from Addis Ababa. Where was out letter of instruction? We would give it him directly. Had we been refused admittance before to the mountain? Certainly not. Rather grudgingly, it appeared, the monk gave orders for one of the debtera to fetch our letter. A rope of plaited thongs was now uncoiled from behind the wicket-gate, and lowered towards us; down this a debtera in a black cape came stealthily climbing, rather like a spider stealthily climbing down its thread towards a fly. He took the crumpled leaf of paper on which Ras Seyum had scribbled the invaluable introduction, kissed the foot of the mountain and reascended; a few minutes later, mollified, it seemed, by the warm words of Ras Seyum, the chief monk gave orders for us to be admitted.

While we were preparing for the rigours of the ascent a troop of white-robed monks appeared from the valley north of the amba. It was astonishing how easily they climbed the rope, two at a time, swinging from their arms lightly like the angels climbing the ladder in Jacob's dream. Like the debtera they took care to kiss the foot of the rock before taking the rope in their strong brown hands; the whole mountain was holy ground, and the ritual kiss corresponded to the kiss bestowed by the pious on the gate-post of a conventional church. All were barefooted, I observed, though some were well enough dressed for one to expect them to be shod; presumably the rules insisted that no shoes were to be worn on such holy ground. Sure enough, as our interpreter prepared to seize the rope, there was a shout of warning from above; shoes must be removed. Accordingly we all removed our shoes and put them in the canvas bag we had with us. A second thong was lowered and the bag was quickly attached and drawn up. A safety thong was now attached to the waist of the interpreter and he followed the bag, climbing the rope with remarkable agility. After him went my companion, more ponderous but safe enough. Then it was my turn.

As I took hold of the main rope I was surprised to find that the monk holding the safety rope was quite prepared to wind me in like a fish, so I went through the motions of climbing but left most of the work to the monk above. In a

Debra Damo, the first mountain of the princes.

solemn voice the story of Debra Damo.

'In the reign of King Gabra Mascal,' he announced ponderously, 'there lived a holy man Aragavi. God had chosen him to be the founder of the monastery, and he sent him a serpent so that he could climb up the amba and build a church on the summit. Aragavi climbed up the serpent like a ladder; and, aided by King Gabra Maskal, he built the church as God directed; and soon there were 6,000 monks on the mountain and 3,000 nuns at its foot, all giving glory to God. When Aragavi became old in years, God sent him a servant named Teklahaimanot, and Teklahaimanot grew rapidly in wisdom, and one day he said he would go to Jerusalem to see the

short time I found myself dangling by the wicket-gate, a foot or two from the end of the rope tied to a wooden bollard hammered into the rock. Ready hands clutched hold of me and I was pulled inside the wicket-gate.

The summit of the amba is about half a mile in diameter, a grassy tableland on which there is ample room for a church and quite a little village of monastic buildings. We were led across this pleasant sward and set down in the shade of a fig tree to wait while the Mamre or Abbot himself was being summoned. The monk in the canary-coloured cape was apparently the Prior of the monastery. I took the opportunity offered by this little respite to ask him about the history of the mountain. After a little encouragement – I believe I took his photograph – he began to tell us in a

Garden of Gethesmane and the hill of blood, that is called Golgotha. But Shaitan (Satan) planned to stop Teklahaimanot going on his journey to the Holy Land, and he cut the rope which led from the rock to the ground just as Teklahaimanot started to climb down. Then God gave Teklahaimanot six wings and he flew down to the valley below,' – here the Prior pointed to one of the bamboula trees growing at the foot of the rock and concluded – 'and from that day onwards Teklahaimanot would fly back and forth to Jerusalem above the clouds like an aeroplane.'

After this picturesque account of the early history of the monastery, I expected an equally picturesque account about the days when the mountain was used as a prison for the King's sons. But the Prior looked blank when I asked him

In a short time I found myself dangling by the wicket-gate, a foot or two from the end of the rope tied to a wooden bollard hammered into the rock.

and mumbled, 'No, this was never a prison; this was a church.' I pressed him further. Did he not know that a rebel Queen called Judith, had surprised the mountain and killed all 400 of the King's sons? The Prior still shook his head. Then his eyes brightened a little, as though remembering something he had heard said long ago. 'Yes,' he said, 'it is true that Judith came to the Mountain, but I do not think that she killed 400 princes; she killed only one man here, and his name was Holofernes.'

Just then the Abbot came hurrying up to greet his visitors. He was dressed in what seemed to be his ceremonial attire – a cape of scarlet brocade across his shoulders, a purple cassock below, while a bevy of altar-boys jostled behind him ringing a bell and waving a large ceremonial umbrella. It was clear that word had got about that the Franks had photographed the Prior, and might be persuaded to take picture of others too. Accordingly I obliged with a series of snapshots. However there were cries of horror as the flash-bulbs flashed in their reflectors; one old priest sank down like St Paul on the road to Damascus, crying out that

he was blinded. He was not to be reassured till I made him a present of the expended bulb. Eventually we were led towards the church concealed behind a mud wall in the centre of the amba.

We were both limping as we reached the church. In our stockinged feet we had walked across a patch of grass thickly sown with thorns. The Abbot observed this, and a debtera who was ready with a pair of tweezers was alerted; clearly the monks themselves must have suffered occasional sore feet. After the offending thorns had been ritually removed, we entered the church precincts. The façade of the church, framed by the dark porch, glowed jewel-like ahead of us, its limestone walls relieved with courses of wood and fitted with the projecting stumps that Ethiopians call 'monkey heads'.

The church of Debra Damo is the earliest of the Christian churches of Ethiopia that now survive. It was built at some time between the sixth and the tenth centuries; in style as well as date it lies somewhere between the pagan obelisks of Axum and the Christian churches of the twelfth century.

By degrees we were admitted to the arcana. First we were shown the narthex or ante-chamber. In its dusty ceiling one could dimly make out a series of wood carvings – peacocks drinking from a vase, a lion and a monkey, and various fabulous animals. These, as I knew, were probably copies from Syrian textiles imported into the country. The designs looked familiar enough – hardly different from the fabulous beasts that decorate our Romanesque churches.

LEFT: *Saint Teklahaimanot sprouts wings after the devil has cut the rope during his climb to Debra Damo.*
RIGHT: *My turn now. I left most of the work to the monk.*

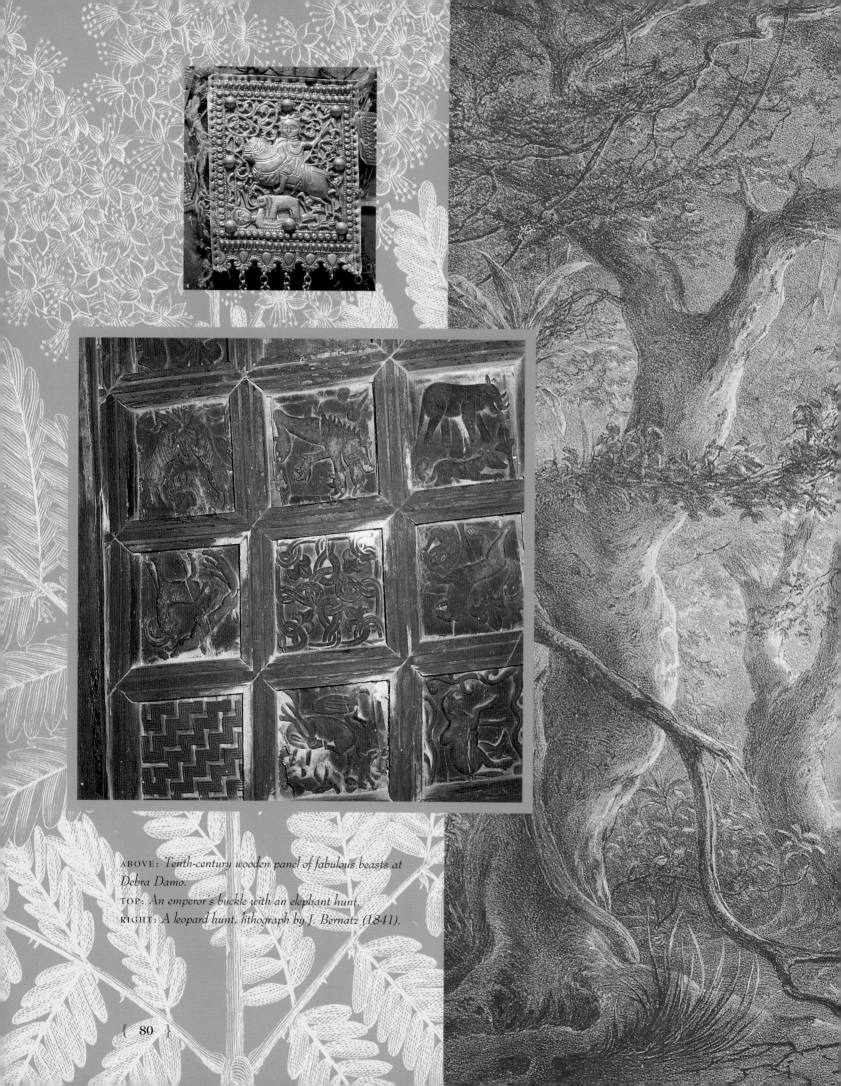

ABOVE: *Tenth-century wooden panel of fabulous beasts at Debra Damo.*

TOP: *An emperor's buckle with an elephant hunt.*

RIGHT: *A leopard hunt, lithograph by J. Bernatz (1841).*

Priests holding processional crosses (LEFT AND CENTRE LEFT) *and small crosses, including a medieval cross carved from olive wood* (CENTRE RIGHT AND RIGHT) *for the faithful to kiss.*

And in fact, as I reflected, the art of Egypt and Syria and Byzantium was developing on similar lines to European art when these panels were being cut. It was a melancholy thought that, ten centuries later, workmanship of this sort is not to be had in Ethiopia.

When we had gained the nave of the church, the full excitement of the architecture was apparent. The stones holding up the roof piers were actual Axumite relics incorporated in the Christian structure; while the doors and windows which held up the roof were all Axumite in style; their knobbly frames were of exactly the same design as those on the obelisks I had seen at Axum. But the demands of the Christian church had produced entirely un-Axumite features. Below the nave roof a 'clerestory' of wooden windows let in a dim religious light from the outside world. And just visible above the ubiquitous draperies that shrouded the church in hieratic gloom, we could see a chancel arch leading to the sanctuary. It was exciting to see, here in this fortress above the wastes of Moslem Africa, features cast in the strong mould of the basilicas of early Christendom. My companion, whose interest in Debra Damo had slackened off

once we had gained the summit, declared he was intrigued by the bizarre scheme of things. 'It's a rum sort of architecture,' he said, 'and I wouldn't have missed it, even if we hadn't had to climb a rope to get here.'

Beyond the nave we were not allowed to go; we were not even allowed a peep at the sanctuary. Anyway, it was high time we were off as we had to be back at Makalle that evening. The hospitable Abbot, however, would not allow us to leave before drinking a glass of 'talla' in the refectory. Despite our protests we were led to a spacious refectory where we were set down on leather chairs and had to wait, corroded by impatience, while the slow ritual of hospitality worked itself out. While we fidgeted the Abbot poured out an interminable tale of woe about the falling revenue of the monastery, the decrease of vocations and broken promises of assistance. 'If only His Imperial Majesty the Emperor would come,' he concluded sadly, 'we would get more money to finish painting the church, as well as a proper road built to the foot of the mountain.' We promised to give the Emperor his message personally as soon as we returned to Addis, and after an infinitely protracted farewell – my companion was now almost hysterical with impatience – we pressed our offering of five dollars into his hand, and ran towards the gate-house above the wicket-gate. A peal of thunder in the north announced that we had no time to spare for our return.

We were soaked to the skin when we staggered to the car several hours afterwards. The amba itself was invisible behind a wall of cloud, intermittently rent by lightning. Later, as we drove southwards out of the valley, the amba stood out in bold relief, the huts of priests just visible on the southern rim, while a watery sun rose over Senafe.

There was exciting news when I returned from this excursion to the South. The Governor-General, Asserate Kassa, was definitely leaving for Gondar that Friday, and he had said he would like to see me again; he could then make the arrangements for the second Wehni expedition in advance of our arrival at Gondar. Later that week, taking one or two photographs of the Mountain to show him, I made the weary climb to the Kassa Ghibbi on Entotto. As before he could hardly have been more hospitable. The photographs, he declared, excited him tremendously; he asked if he could have copies. Certainly I would send them to Gondar. Oh, no, he demurred, no, it would be better for them to stay in Addis. Soon he had steered the conversation away from Addis and Gondar, and was indulging his nostalgic memories of England. When I left after tea I realized that he had said nothing about leaving for Gondar the next day. Perhaps he would be detained for still another week after all. It was maddening. I felt certain that with his galvanic presence at Gondar, success could not elude us.

My own plans crystallized rapidly. A second postcard arrived from Dr Jäger suggesting that we set out on the following weekend. I must arrange the mules and guides myself, but he could borrow a W.H.O. jeep from the hospital. I cabled back that I expected to arrive on Monday – which allowed me three days to collect the climbing rope from the embassy, various extra pieces of equipment for my camera from a photographer's, an 'explorer's suit' from the Armenian tailors, and to renew my visa at the Ministry of Interior. As I might have guessed the first four tasks were completed in a morning, while the visa hunt took five days. I arrived at Gondar on the cargo plane on the Wednesday. But if I was behind schedule Asserate Kassa had lagged still further behind. He had still not reached Gondar when Dr Jäger and I drove off towards Belesa on Friday morning. If he was to help me now, it would be on my third expedition. But I began to doubt whether he would ever come at all.

THE ASCENT OF DEBRA DAMO

The Return to the Mountain

Are there no weeds and bogs and rivers in your country? What have you to do with that damned Nile, where he rises or whether he rises at all or not?

Bruce's servant becomes impatient
with his master's explorations

For the second Wehni expedition we had chosen a new route; we had no time to spare, and we believed it shorter.

On Bruce's map the road to the Mountain was indicated by a dotted line drawn eastwards from the main road running south-east from Gondar to Lake Tana. We had roughly followed this route on our first expedition; we had left our truck at Tuesday Market where the road forked, and struck out eastwards by mule towards Belesa. But in Bruce's narrative the Mountain was twice described as being close to Enfras, the King's summer palace on the lake. I understood from Colonel Tamarat that Enfras was still a sizeable village today – though quite unmarked on any of the British or Italian maps – and Dr Jäger agreed with my suggestion that if we pressed on by car beyond Tuesday Market to Enfras, the mule trip into the Mountains would be correspondingly shorter, and the journey itself shorter on balance. The plan seemed to work well, as the local governor of Enfras, Dejazmatch Kasai, was a patient of Dr Jäger's and had invited him to pay him a visit at any time. A messenger had been sent ahead of us a day before and returned with the message that he would be delighted to see us on our way, that his own mules and servants would be ours. I was particularly glad to hear this as I did not want to have to bother Colonel Tamarat again with requests for guides and mules. And I was particularly keen to meet the Dejazmatch. His grandfather was none other then the famous or infamous Kasai who rose from being a small-time brigand to sitting on the throne of the King of Kings; he is known to history as the tragic Emperor Theodore who degenerated from a zealous reformer into a bigoted tyrant and who finally took his own life in 1868 when besieged by the British Army under Napier at Magdala.

The three of us – Dr Jäger, myself and a young Ethiopian medical student who had volunteered to accompany us to act as interpreter – were received by Dejazmatch Kasai as soon as we reached Enfras. He was about sixty, I should imagine, white-haired, extremely fine-looking in a European way; he was dressed in what I knew to be normal Governor's uniform – a Burberry with topee and brogues. He was accompanied by his son of about twelve who wore a gaberdine suit, gym shoes and carried an amulet round his neck to protect him from nose-bleeds, as he told us. He led us to a brand-new hut in the centre of Enfras. Its roof was thatched, but its sides were open like a marquee, and a pine-scented breeze blew through the apertures; down here at the level of Lake Tana, a bare 6,000 feet, one began to feel the heat. Soon we were seated in the grateful shade of this marquee and drank 'tej' or mead and ate a volcanic Ethiopian dish of 'wat'. Our host withdrew discreetly to a hut for the simpler meal which the Friday fast demanded of the pious.

The Dejazmatch returned after lunch and took a glass of whisky. Dr Jäger turned to the subject of mules. Had he been able to hire some of us? We would, of course, like to pay. Indeed he had mules, he replied, but we were his guests; he would give us his own riding mule if it was necessary. There was nothing we need pay for. Dr Jäger whispered to me that we must make some sort of payment later. A servant was sent to fetch the guides and saddle up the mules. He himself prepared to return to his own house which was a mile or so away. We thanked him for arranging everything so well, and he bowed inscrutably and left us.

Three seedy-looking mules, one already lame, were now brought out of a hut; each had its accompanying halo of flies. There were no pack-mules at all. Our guide-to-be, who had the title of Barambas – denoting the lowest rank in the Ethiopian scale of honours – announced sullenly that he might be able to find two donkeys. Two spavined donkeys were produced after a prolonged argument.

The luggage we had brought was now unloaded from the jeep. Dr Jäger had brought a large suitcase and innumerable small plastic bags that bore the proud names of international airline companies; as well as my knapsack and the great coil of climbing rope, I had brought a safari camp-bed, an extra kit-bag of clothes and food, and an aluminium tiffin-carrier full of mincemeat lent to me by the Anglo-Indian

with whom I was staying at Gondar; Mr Lema, the medical student, was the least prodigal of luggage space, bringing only a light bag and a mackintosh, but Dr Jäger had given him charge of a five-gallon jerry-can of drinking water. Together our luggage made an impressive pyramid as it lay piled up on the ground. We loaded up; the five-gallon can of drinking water found the last place on top of the quivering pyramid. As the donkeys set off from Enfras towards the plateau to the north, they were almost invisible under their burdens.

We now turned to the mules. I could not believe that the lame one would support either of us more than a mile or two on the flat, let alone on a thirty-mile ride up nearly 4,000 feet of mountain. The other two looked stronger, but pawed the ground threateningly. With what my companions took to be self-sacrifice I chose the lame one. We all mounted. The Ethiopian harness was new to both Dr Jäger and me. We

adjusted ourselves awkwardly to the bony wooden saddle with backrest and pommel, and gingerly took the reins which were joined in a loop close by the mule's long, donkey-like ears. The stirrups which are made for riding barefooted, with the side of the stirrup held between first and second toe, were abominably narrow; luckily we both wore gym shoes, but Mr Lema, who was built like a footballer and wore boots, had to ride with his legs dangling. The little cavalcade jogged along the track away from Enfras following the donkeys. Wehni was some hours ahead – three hours? four hours? five hours? nobody knew – and we kept our small talk for the evening when we should be there. Perhaps we were all a little dispirited.

The track led first through high grass in a broad valley with warka and zana trees dotted about its flanks. We forded a river called the Garno. Its inane meandering brought us to its banks a second time higher up; we splashed through its

THE RETURN TO THE MOUNTAIN

*Our luggage made an impressive
pyramid on the ground. But
could the donkeys carry it?*

brown pools again and hurried on. The donkeys, to our surprise, still kept their lead; no doubt the Barambas was whipping them on. My own mule was also a source of some astonishment. As soon as we had left Enfras it had stopped limping and was now going excellently. Its peculiar tripping gait, giving the impression that it was walking on high-heeled shoes, was rather congenial to me. I congratulated myself on my choice. Both Dr Jäger and Mr Lema were having trouble with their mounts, which had mastered the art of gently brushing them against thorn trees, as though they were parasites which might be persuaded to drop off if presented with a suitable alternative.

We caught up with the donkeys eventually in a narrow valley remarkable for a tall pinnacle of rock called Guramba. I remembered seeing it from the great Belesa tableland; it was then a needle of rock lost in the misty foothills towards the lake. Now it towered over us, perhaps half the height of Wehni, though much slimmer. At its foot the fields were green and grassy and there were palm trees in plenty. Already we had left the crackly, dry plains of the Tana littoral, and the air was cooler. The Barambas led us ever upward. His appearance, however, did not inspire confidence – he was a chubby, bald man and had the roguish look of the bald-headed satyrs who chase maenads round Greek vases.

By the time we had reached the level of the long-leaved rhododendron-like plants called argagaffa, I felt all the moroseness of the afternoon evaporate. Dr Jäger announced that he too felt happier. Mr Lema jogged amicably behind. The sun grew ever lower, as we ascended, dismounting occasionally for the steepest paths, or the shingly terracing where the mules seemed likely to slip. Once we came to a place where the Barambas, with what I thought was excessive courtesy, consulted Mr Lema as well as his companions on the route we should take. I was glad to observe he disregarded the advice; I knew Mr Lema to be a perfect stranger to the area. Dr Jäger and I rode merrily on. We began to find the wooden saddles perfectly agreeable, though we looked forward eagerly to the moment when we should be able to cease declaring how agreeable they were.

About an hour before sunset the Barambas halted. We had reached a particularly sylvan valley below a series of wooded buttresses which supported the southward thrust of the tableland. He waited for us to come up with him and then began a long jibber-jabber of Amharic. 'Perhaps he is eulogizing the scenery,' said Dr Jäger. Mr Lema corrected him with a short translation. 'He asks you the way, doctor; he says he came this way long ago but cannot remember now which is the path to Wehni. I think he is afraid to admit we are lost.' And lost we were. There was no one about to ask; the valley, fertile as it was, seemed uninhabited. The maps of the area were of no help at all as their information was mostly hearsay and sometimes frankly myth; none of the contours indicated on the map corresponded to those of the terrain we had seen or could see ahead; and our schoolboy's compass gave us no help at all in consequence. All we could do was climb to the tableland and hope we had not deviated too much east or west of Wehni. According to schedule we were to be at the Mountain by that evening, attempt the ascent the next day, which was Saturday, and be back on the afternoon of the Sunday at Enfras. It was an absurdly unelastic schedule, but Dr Jäger's work at the hospital would allow no other. With the fecklessness of the Barambas the chances of success were now seriously decreased.

It was dark when we reached the tableland. For the last few miles we had groped our way across a series of tangled ravines, with only the incentive of the camp ahead to spur us on. The mules were very tired, and we had to dismount more often; the donkeys had finally fallen behind, and were, we hoped, somewhere in the valleys below following our trail. Whenever we came to a clearing in the undergrowth Dr Jäger suggested we stop and set up camp. I explained that the Barambas and his companions would never allow us to halt away from a village, with good reason. They had brought nothing with them, not even any unleavened Ethiopian bread, injerra, to eat, and had nothing but their shammas to protect them against the cold. We pressed sadly onwards, feeling the hairy touch of briars and liana on our faces. The first bats of evening shrieked dismally in the gloaming, and my luminous white mule assumed a sinister spectral look as it jogged wearily on ahead of me up the shadowy track.

The village we reached at last was couched on a grassy platform ambiguously poised between valley and tableland, and was shrouded in the rich, almost fungus-like vegetation that grew where the streams poured off the plateau. Dark as it was I noticed a copse of the rare and romantic kosso tree. I would be glad of an opportunity to study it next morning. For the moment we sat on a mossy bank in an ecstasy of exhaustion. We had been riding ever since lunch-time and had climbed nearly 4,000 feet.

When I had got my breath back I began to take stock of our predicament. There was no sign of the donkeys in the valley up which we had come, not even an echo of the faint bird-like cries which the two donkey-drivers had emitted at intervals to keep in touch with the Barambas. They must have missed their way in the dusk, and climbed to the tableland by a different route. Either that or the donkeys had collapsed completely, and their drivers had stopped for the night in some village far below us. In either case, the prospects for us were not pleasant, as the two donkeys carried all we possessed – tents, food, clothes, cameras, everything. I asked Dr Jäger what he thought: he smiled sleepily, blissfully remote from the problem. The Barambas had not waited for consultations, but had disappeared into the village huts ahead of us; no doubt he was now carousing with the headman. I did not regret his leaving us as I was heartily sick of the man. In an ugly frame of mind I climbed into my sleeping-bag which had remained with me as a cushion between the bony back of the mule and the spiky wooden framework on which the saddle was slung. I was not surprised to observe a moment later a theatrical flash of lightning flicker over the valley up which we had come, and to feel several drops of thundery rain rattle like lead pellets on the quilting of my bag. It was just the right moment to be caught in a tropical thunderstorm.

But in the interval between the lightning and the answering rolls of thunder, I heard a grateful sound echo in the valley, the faint cry of 'Shibera, shibera', the call of one donkey-driver to the other. 'It's the donkeys at last,' I told Dr Jäger excitedly. In the darkness I felt he was gently smiling as he replied that he had never doubted it. 'They'll just arrive in time,' he added as he turned over and dozed off again.

The donkeys did indeed reach us before the rain began in earnest. In a trice two limbs of acacia wood were cut and trimmed into tent-poles, the luggage hustled into safety, as the tent rose unsteadily to its feet like a balloon slowly filling

with gas; with the last guy-rope disentangled from the ankles of Mr Lema, and the pegs hammered into place between two boulders, we threw ourselves in after the luggage, and lay there panting in the sticky darkness.

Instinctively each of us took some urgent task and made it our own. A mellow light flickered in one corner of the tent where Dr Jäger was shielding the fragile frame of a candle set up on a marmalade tin; the rain had begun to pour on to my sleeping-bag through one of the star-shaped holes torn in the fabric of the tent, so I sat like the Dutch boy with my finger in the hole; Mr Lema held the slim poles we had so hastily cut, and braced them against the force of the wind. Later, when the thunderstorm degenerated into a steady drizzle, we reverted to our natural selves, looking slightly sheepishly at each other as though we had acted too theatrically in the crisis; this feeling of bathos was confirmed when we heard the Barambas' two companions chatting amicably outside and the crackle of sticks burning; they must have sat there through the worst of the tempest. Dr Jäger's candle eventually went out, and we lay quietly in the darkness. Stars were visible through the holes in the tent walls. It was going to be a crisp frosty night. I felt for the tiffin-carrier and began to eat the mince noisily in the darkness, feeling as I lay there on the sweet-smelling wet grass like some exotic ruminant.

I was woken next morning by the gentle, regular noise of the village nearby; the dull thump of a pestle and mortar pounding berberi, the insect-like murmur of conversation, the slow rasp of 'teff' being ground between two flat stones,

LEFT: *The Gondar-style palace of Gazara near Enfras from where I launched my second expedition to the Mountain.*

BELOW: *The Barambas surveys our route. We were soon hopelessly lost.*

and the subdued noise of chanting in the church of Michael. I peered through the tent-flap. The sun had just reached our green dell, throwing a fiercely theatrical light on to the surrounding trees. The kossos were looking extravagantly, almost agonizingly romantic: their leaves projected like green fangs; their mottled yellow bark was scaly and reptilian; their purple blossoms hung down like clusters of over-ripe grapes.

The kosso tree is not, alas, peculiar to Ethiopia as is often said; known as *Hagenia abyssinica* it is also found in the mountain fastnesses of Imatonga in the Sudan and the Ruwenzori in Uganda. But it was, at any rate, discovered in Ethiopia first, the discovery being made by Bruce, who came to admire it above all trees. I too lost my heart to the kosso; just as the blue gum symbolized the shanty-town and the motor-road, the purple-flowering kosso symbolized for me the secret places of the deep country. It is sad that for Ethiopians this romantic tree has the most unromantic associations. Its bark is used as a specific against tape-worms.

After breakfast from our separate stores of food, we climbed the last few hundred feet to the tableland. The

unhappy truth, long suspected, was now clear; we had taken a sharp turn to the west during the afternoon and had lost all we had gained by the new route; indeed we had blundered almost to the exact point we had reached by the first evening of the first expedition. Hardly a mile ahead of us was the village of Mender Mariam, with its eponymous amba. This was most disheartening. However, in the clear, rain-washed morning it was impossible to be depressed for long. The tableland was now looking even lusher than the previous month; the deep grass was worked with small violets and plants of traveller's joy, so that it reminded Dr Jäger of a piece of oriental brocade; the dust had been washed off the thatch roofs and wattle corrals of the village around us; the coats of the sheep looked noticeably glossier. It was clear that the rainstorm the previous night had been preceded by several others just as severe. It was to be expected, of course, that the tableland should enjoy different weather from the low land round Gondar. Perhaps the Little Rains, which are supposed to reach Gondar in March, precipitated on this long projecting tumulus of land a month or two earlier.

Taking a route along the southern rim of the tableland, we made good time. After an hour we came to a small village called Chahara, dominated by what seemed a very old church of Georghis. We dismounted and crept into the churchyard, a grassy ring encircled by stately junipers as usual. The church itself was locked, and there was no sign of a priest or sexton; but the churchyard was spectacularly beautiful, perhaps more so than any other I saw in Ethiopia. Several dead junipers, half fallen, had arranged themselves like ogive windows in the dark green wall around us. Through these massy cathedral windows the view of the lake, the littoral and the great buttresses of foothills broke dizzily upon us. I was able to make out the heraldic, porpoise-like shape of the lake and identify the individual islands as far as Chircos; while the palace of Gazara, near Enfras, seemed almost within hailing distance. While we were standing in the churchyard an old man appeared and we asked if there were any pictures in the church. He replied gravely that there were none and that anyway the priest had left for Michael Debra earlier that morning as it was market day.

The church of Michael Debra stood as I remembered it on a wooded knoll, with the rude huts of the village

scattered about the brown plain below. But the character of the place had changed entirely. Today it was a scene of almost frenzied activity; while the paths radiating out along the plain to the neighbouring villages were crowded with donkey caravans like lines of hurrying termites. As we approached we were able to distinguish all the usual paraphernalia of country markets: the wicker bins of the 'teff', which was probably exported from this lush tableland to the lowlands around; and ingots of salt which would have come hundreds of miles across the highlands from the outer deserts, increasing in price as they went; in even the most remote area salt is an essential import. We dismounted to look at the other excitements. There were pyramids of grain, chickens which were still alive but trussed head downwards across a donkey's saddle, bundles of onions, and, what was a surprise to find in such a remote place, a single large bar of Lifebuoy carbolic soap. I inquired the price of this luxury import. The market woman sternly replied that it was not for sale; she had reserved it for the local governor. We all giggled boorishly at this piece of information.

At the height of our mirth the Barambas shuffled forward and made a remarkable announcement. 'We have brought you here as we promised,' he said gravely, 'Now we shall return to Enfras.'

'But this wasn't the agreement ...'

'We are sorry, we are returning to Enfras as was agreed.'

We tried argument, cajolery, threats, even bribes; Dr Jäger offered quite a number of dollars to them. The Barambas was adamant. He had been told to take us to Michael Debra, we had arrived and here he was leaving us. To show he meant it the Barambas swiftly unloaded the donkeys, and took our sleeping-bags from under the mules' saddles. They lay in five foolish heaps on the ground in the shade of the acacia trees.

An hour had passed and the Barambas was still adamant, though there was apparently no other means of our reaching Wehni than with his mules. 'Now we are stranded,' said Dr Jäger quietly, and so we were.

Our expedition, which had never constituted a very full-blooded attempt on the Mountain – for this I naturally blamed only myself – had become a fiasco. However, at

this critical moment one of the market-goers, a man of about forty with a badly swollen face, whom I remembered seeing at Wehni, came forward and spoke earnestly to Mr Lema, who brightened at the information. 'This man is from Wehni,' he announced. 'He says that last night the Governor of Addis Zemen – that's the next village along the road after Enfras – arrived at the amba. Apparently Colonel Tamarat had telephoned to ask him to meet us there. Perhaps he is still there waiting for us. Let us send a messenger quickly to tell him that we are stranded here at Michael Debra, and he will come here and rescue us.'

This seemed an admirable plan to all of us; the Barambas, too, seemed eager to meet the Governor, and to explain his position. A messenger was soon found. The man with the swollen face presented himself as a candidate; he would run there in an hour if we paid him. We promised two Ethiopian dollars – two days' wages – and after Dr Jäger had given him an aspirin for his swollen face as a sort of advance, he set off for Wehni at a cracking pace. 'He'll bust if he goes on like that,' I observed to Dr Jäger. 'He's going to die anyway,' said Dr Jäger in his gentlest voice, 'he's got a form of bone tumour, I think.' The messenger ran blithely on down the well-remembered track to Wehni, till he disappeared beyond the ridge which excluded the Mountain and the Happy Valley as surely from our sight as though we had been still at Gondar.

Two more hours had passed. It was now nearly sunset and our messenger had not returned. The Barambas and his men, and Mr Lema too, had left us for a tukal in the village. We sat together under the acacia trees on the knoll above the village and listlessly ate the packed meals we had brought – for Dr Jäger processed gruyère sandwiches, and for me the unending mince which Mr Rams' tiffin-carrier poured out like a horn of plenty.

Suddenly there was a stir in the village below, and a confused jibber-jabber of voices floated up to us in the clear air. 'It's the rescue party,' I told Dr Jäger, hardly believing it myself. And so it was. When we looked through Dr Jäger's field-glasses we could see what the sharp eyes of the villagers had seen unaided – a seemingly endless file of men was unwinding over the ridge above Wehni. Nine, ten, eleven ...

we shouted the glorious news to Mr Lema ... nineteen, twenty, twenty-one ... I knew now what the men on the walls of Lucknow and Mafeking must have felt when they saw the relief column.

As they trotted towards us we began to make out the details. Riding at the head of the column was our messenger who had somehow borrowed a mule; he was looking tremendously pleased with himself. Behind him were a posse of armed men, including one who carried a Bren gun on his shoulder, and a cavalcade of no less than nine mounted men. The local Governor himself was not at first conspicuous, as all the riders wore the same grade of topee. But soon I noticed that one of the tallest and at the same time youngest of the men wore a pair of binoculars slung round his neck; on the analogy of the Governor of Belesa possessing just such a pair, I assumed he was the Governor, and I was right. When the front of the column was about twenty paces away he dismounted and walked ahead of the others towards me, with a confident and eager expression on his handsome, brown face.

To greet our rescuer I stepped forward in what I hoped was the best Livingstone manner. We bowed to each other at about ten paces, we bowed again at five, then we shook hands and bowed a third time. Dr Jäger and Mr Lema then shambled up, and the rescue column crowded round us, all talking and gesticulating in a more Latin than Ethiopian way. When silence was restored the Governor delivered a short speech of welcome.

Both Dr Jäger and I, already in an emotional frame of mind because of our situation, were sincerely moved by this speech. I was endeavouring to reply when a boy of about twelve came shyly up to me and offered first me, and then Dr Jäger, a small posy of Alpine flowers, marigolds and crocuses, and a spray of wild thyme and rosemary. This entirely unmanned me. We had blundered like schoolboys into his private paradise; we had failed to arrive on the appointed day, got ourselves stranded and then sent a messenger peremptorily asking for rescue; hot-foot he had come and this was our reward – not recriminations but flowers culled from the Happy Valley. (No other valley, I well knew, could have yielded such fertile treasure.) I stood there clutching the damp posy in my sweating hands, abandoning myself to

... we had failed to arrive on the appointed day, got ourselves stranded and then sent a messenger peremptorily asking for rescue; hot-foot he had come and this was our reward – not recriminations but flowers culled from the Happy Valley. I stood there clutching the damp posy in my sweating hands, abandoning myself to the moment, more moving, I think in retrospect, than any in all the months of my wandering. They have become the symbol for me of my love affair with the Mountain.

THE RETURN TO THE MOUNTAIN

broke we reached Mender Mariam.

That evening, as we lay snugly ensconced in the tent, while the storm crashed and thundered above us, the Governor, who proved to be a Fitarawi, slipped in to pay us a visit. 'Why don't you try to climb the Mountain?' he asked us, grinning. 'I think I could have got up if I'd had your rope.' I explained that Dr Jäger had to be back at his hospital on Monday morning. The Fitarawi made a wry face. 'Well, you must come later – here's my visiting card.' I was handed a bilingual card which I slipped between the pages of my Bruce for safety. (I was most surprised, I must confess, to get a card: I only saw one other Ethiopian with a visiting card and he was a Minister in Addis.) We fell to talking of the country which he administered. On the thorny topic of shiftas he was unusually frank. His own territory was free of them, he was sure of this. 'Why do you carry a Bren gun then?' I asked. 'It's a matter of honour now,' he replied, 'though two years ago we needed it for actual protection.' His last command in Begemdir was not so fortunate, however. 'You still get shiftas in Gaint,' he told me. 'They are hard people there. I shouldn't advise you to travel there without an armed escort.' I questioned him closely about this Gaint, as Stephen Wright had told me it was the area most likely to have a cache of churches still surviving unrecorded. Did he know any very old churches in Gaint? The Fitarawi was surprisingly knowledgeable about the churches throughout the country. We talked for an hour about some I knew and some I had heard of; others in Gaint that were quite new names to me – in particular a church called Bethlehem.

the moment, more moving, I think in retrospect, than any in all the months of my wandering. Even today, when the remnants of those once fragrant flowers lie dusty in a cupboard like bones in an ossuary, I can hardly look upon them with equanimity. They have become the symbol for me of my love affair with the Mountain. Like a love-letter, brown with age, they still hold the power to make my heart leap with pain and joy to remember the green tableland of Belesa, the valley and the Mountain which in a curious way have become part of me.

For the first few miles we rode ceremoniously back along the plateau. Then, as the evening thunder rolled ever more insistently, we quickened our pace. Our sedate retreat soon became a rout. The new mules provided by the Governor's cavalcade – three of his nine men had dismounted to give us their mules – were magnificent beasts, and when our bugler blew a blast on his horn to encourage us, they pricked up their long donkey's ears like hunters in the shires at the sound of the hunting horn, and we flew along over the springy turf. The man with the Bren gun was hard put to it to keep up. Just before the storm

4 Chapter Four

The fifteenth-century Book of
Gospels that first put me on the
trail of the unrecorded church at
Bethlehem. This page shows the
Holy Family in The Flight into
Egypt.

Ghosts

**I spent a fortnight after my return
from Belesa maundering around the
town of Gondar. In my previous visit I
had hardly given the town a glance;
my eyes had been for the crisply
restored ruins within the palace
compound. Now I turned with
increasing excitement to the shabby,
half-ruinous, creepy provincial town
that rubbed shoulders with the
Gondar of the Kings.**

Gondar, the town, is a ghost from the days of the Italian
experiment in Ethiopia. The Italians selected the town as a
suitable place for one of their largest provincial capitals. It
enjoyed a salubrious climate, lay in the centre of the best
farming country, and possessed a picturesque cache of
palaces which appealed to the more historically minded
heirs of Caesar. The Italians proceeded to build a
stupendous road to Gondar from Asmara, and plan a new
town of a European type to adjoin the old. A broad piazza, a
long corso from this piazza to the palace, a main street
spiralling down to the plain like the road from some
Umbrian hill-town, a city centre of multi-storied blocks to
house the offices of the administration, and a rash of stone
bungalows to house the garrison and colonists – these
were as soon planned as executed. In less than three years,
a complete modern town had arisen on the grassy ridge to
the north of the palaces, which became the showpiece of
the new empire. Then the war came. The Axis forces made
Gondar the rallying-point for their defence of Abyssinia
against the British and Commonwealth troops. It was
here that there was the bitterest fighting of the whole
campaign.

Nowadays the piazza presents a ghostly scene. For
hours at a time the vast concave square may be empty – all
except for the skeletons of motor-cars that nobody has
thought fit to remove. The corso, too, is empty, but for a few
strollers who peer idly into the gloomy shopping arcades
where turbaned Yemeni deal in Japanese hardware and
Indian calico. Then along come a couple of gharries
clattering down the pitted road with lame irregular hoof-

beats; their drivers carry whips which are forbidden in Addis
on humanitarian grounds. Occasionally there is a small
cavalcade of market-goers or even – though this I saw only
once – a posse of prisoners wearing leg-irons and going
under heavy guard to the local assize court.

After a fortnight of tranquil days in Gondar I felt braced for
the rigours of the deep country once more. Though I had not
given up hope of conquering the Mountain, I had for the
moment plans in another direction.

On the disastrous last trip to Wehni the Fitarawi had
inspired me with the idea of setting out to look for medieval
churches in the province of Gaint, that lay far to the east of
Gondar. This was, like Belesa, *terra incognita* – country
unmapped and unexplored by any Europeans; even Stephen
Wright had never visited Gaint. I spent some time in the Fasil
Ghibbi, and about the churches of Gondar exploring
possibilities. All the evidence seemed to suggest that Gaint
was the sort of place where discoveries might be made.
There were numerous manuscripts exhibited in the Fasil
Ghibbi which had been lent by churches in Gaint; some were
certainly medieval; the finest of all came from a church in
Gaint called Bethlehem. Now Bethlehem was the name of the
church that the Fitarawi had singled out as being particularly
old. Putting the two pieces of evidence together, it seemed
well worth making an expedition through Gaint with
Bethlehem the principal objective.

Colonel Tamarat was as helpful as could be. Debra
Tabor was the nearest we could get by road to Gaint; he
promised to arrange with the Governor of Debra Tabor for
me to have an escort who would both guard me and
interpret for me. And he arranged for me to meet a Barambas
who worked in the municipality and claimed to have visited
the church of Bethlehem.

The interview was unfortunately short and inconclusive.
The chief distinguishing mark of medieval churches is that
they are rectangular in plan, with a flat roof, while since the
Moslem wars of the sixteenth century churches have been
circular in plan with a conical roof, just like the tukals.

'Is the church square?' I asked.

'Oh, yes, the church is square.'

'Not round like other churches?'

the country; or so I thought.

However, on the day before I was to leave for Debra Tabor I met someone who was to change the whole course of the expedition.

I was walking along the stony Via del Popolo when I observed ahead a knot of people, gathered together in the middle of the road, pushing and shoving to see something in their midst. I imagined that there had been some sort of accident; the gharries often collided on the hills and occasionally the occupants were thrown out and injured. A very strange noise was seeping out from the centre of the gathering; it must be, I thought, the noise of someone horribly hurt. I hurried up, and pushed my way past the gaping crowd. Beyond them was an inner ring of ragged children, and in the centre of them all, a large bespectacled European. He was uninjured. He was dancing a sort of jig, and while he danced he recited a sort of nonsense rhyme that I learnt as a child from a German governess. His audience eyed this remarkable performance with anxious wonderment, not yet certain whether this stranger's powers were for good or evil.

When the European saw me he stopped the jig abruptly, rose to his feet, dusted his clothes – he wore a sort of rough gaberdine costume, and a wide-awake – and said rather sheepishly, '*Quelquefois il faut faire le buffon pour gagner la confiance des gens-ci,*' repeating this remark in German, Italian and English to make certain that he was understood. Then he introduced himself, and led me to the bar in the piazza. He was apparently an Alsatian ethnologist, a certain Professor Stomf. I had heard about him in Addis. In half an hour I was so under the spell of this remarkable man that I had agreed to take him on my journey to Bethlehem.

'Oh yes, it is round, too.'

This was clearly impossible, but before we could plump with any certainty for one or the other the Barambas had unfortun-ately been called away on a sewage disposal problem and I was left with the crucial question unanswered.

All the other preparations went smoothly forward. I bought extra photographic accessories from the one European shop in Gondar, a chemist's, which stocked everything from penicillin to chocolate bon-bons; I stocked up with tinned foods from an Arab store and I bought a number of petty remedies against disease that might come in useful. I was now all set for a fortnight's wandering in

To Bethlehem

We flew south to Debra Tabor next morning. I had chosen to go by aeroplane not only because it was quicker and hardly more expensive than by lorry, but because the air service had just been inaugurated; this was only the second scheduled flight to Debra Tabor, and I suspected that the landing might prove interesting.

Travellers like poets are mostly an angry race; by flying into a daily fit of passion I proved to the Governor and his son that I was in earnest.

Richard Burton: *First Footsteps in East Africa*

We flew south to Debra Tabor next morning. I had chosen to go by aeroplane not only because it was quicker and hardly more expensive than by lorry, but because the air service had just been inaugurated; this was only the second scheduled flight to Debra Tabor, and I suspected that the landing might prove interesting.

Debra Tabor lies on a lofty ridge of the highlands ringing Lake Tana and is connected by a neck of land to the lower slopes of Mount Guna to the east. At an altitude of some 10,000 feet it must be one of the highest airstrips in all Africa to be served by a regular airline. I asked the American pilot of our Dakota – almost all the pilots of Ethiopian Airlines are Americans seconded from its parent company TWA – whether they had any difficulty landing or taking off.

'It's a bit dicey when there's a cross-wind,' he replied, 'and we had some difficulty in finding the place the first time. But now the missionary's fixed up some markers to guide us in.'

We were soon planing in over a brown and green patchwork of fields and villages. The pilot throttled back as confidently as though we were at Idlewild, and the plane touched down in a long, dusty convex field. As I had hoped, a stream of frenzied villagers raced across the field towards us and solidified round the aeroplane, when we halted, in a mass of anxious, upturned faces. The door of the Dakota was flung open and I stepped out like a Greek god from a machine.

This dramatic introduction to Debra Tabor did not, however, set the scene for the next few days. Though we were most hospitably entertained by the missionary – he was a Seventh Day Adventist from Denmark with a charming wife and family – Debra Tabor proved to be as desolate and forbidding a spot as I ever saw in Ethiopia.

I was relieved when the letter to the local Governor, which had been given me by Colonel Tamarat, finally bore fruit. A ruffianly-looking muleteer was found who promised to hire us two mules and two pack-mules; a police-sergeant, who spoke Italian, and two men under him were allotted to us as guides and escort. On the third day after our arrival we set out shortly after dawn towards the long dorsal ridge of Mount Guna behind which lay the promised land of Gaint.

We left Debra Tabor by the main caravan route across the highlands which runs for nearly 200 miles eastwards to Dessie. The caravan route was unmistakable: the grassy plateau was cut by a number of parallel tracks, worn by the tireless march of mules, donkeys and pedestrians, to which no doubt the seasonal rains added their contribution. Often the paths crossed each other, and sometimes one would diverge from the rest, like a branch line leaving the main railway-track.

Professor Stomf trotted along beside me on a white mule. His chunky frame was encased in a sort of baggy grey suit like an early motoring-costume or a siren-suit; his craggy face was capped by a broad-brimmed canvas hat; he wore mountaineering boots with thick rubber soles. Most of his luggage was contained in a cowhide injerra-bag which he had slung jauntily across his shoulder. 'I've brought candles for the priests, of course,' he announced genially, 'and some peppermints for the children – otherwise only the barest necessities.' Rather to my shame I observed the heavily laden pack-mule containing my own camp-bed, tent, and other camping kit.

As we went Professor Stomf began to expound what he called his mission in Ethiopia. 'We must study people as they are,' he announced, 'not as we choose to make them. It's no good bullying people if you want to find out how they live. Once you take a firm line – pouff –' Professor Stomf made a violent gesture in the air which threatened to capsize the mule.

I soon began to understand what this policy of laissez-faire entailed. A few miles from Debra Tabor the main caravan trail made a wide detour ahead of us; it wound away to the west to a village with a church of Georghis, leaving the highest ridge of the plateau; and then painfully regained the ridge several miles farther on. The direct track was only a single brown furrow in the grassy downs. When Dessime and the muleteer opted for the main trail, I asked if we need

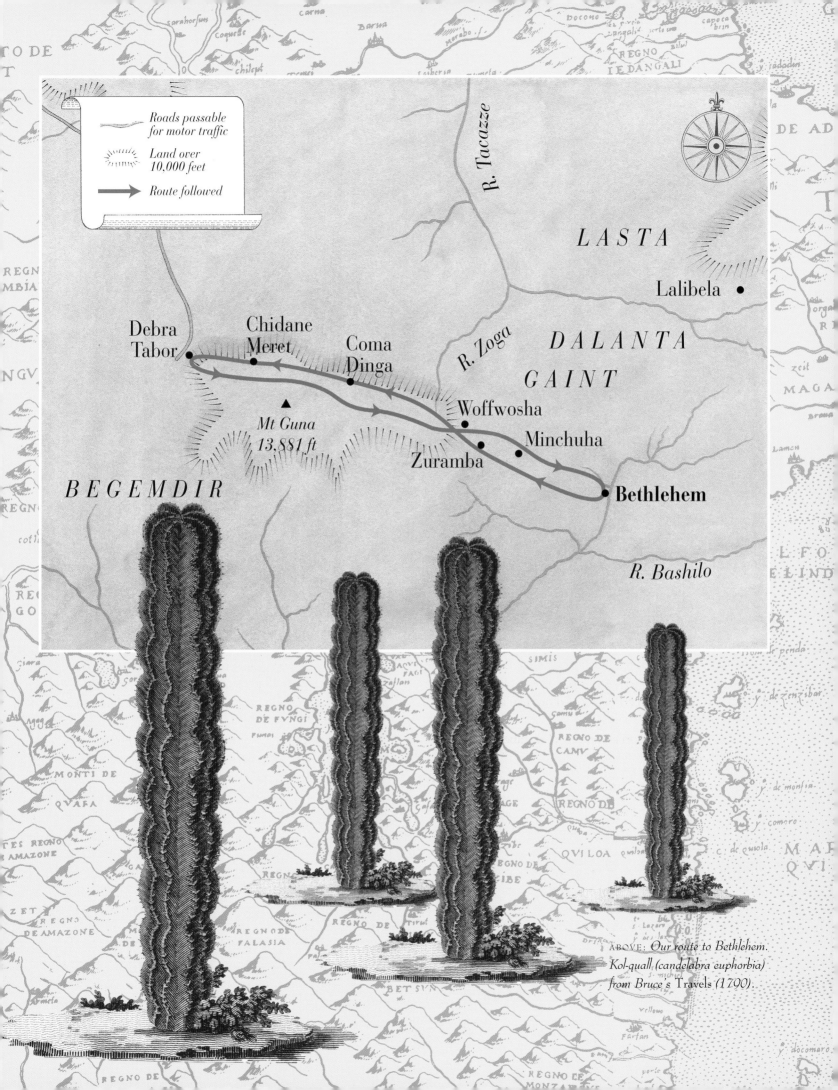

Roads passable for motor traffic

Land over 10,000 feet

Route followed

R. Tacazze

LASTA

Lalibela

R. Zoga

DALANTA

GAINT

Debra Tabor

Chidane Meret

Coma Dinga

Woffwosha

Minchuha

▲

Mt Guna 13,881 ft

Zuramba

Bethlehem

BEGEMDIR

R. Bashilo

ABOVE: *Our route to Bethlehem. Kol-quall (candelabra euphorbia) from Bruce's Travels (1790).*

'I've brought candles for the priests, of course,' he announced genially, 'and some peppermints for the children – otherwise only the barest necessities.' Rather to my shame I observed the heavily laden pack-mule containing my own camp-bed, tent, and other camping kit.

make the detour; I was certain from what I had heard in Debra Tabor that there was nothing to see in this village. Dessime replied that it was always safer to follow the main trail; perhaps there was a river ahead we could not ford. Professor Stomf agreed with him and we took the main trail. 'I'm sorry if this is a bore for you,' he confided to me after a moment. 'I know that there's nothing in the village for us, but they've probably got their reasons for the detour. We must study them as they are, remember.' He grinned good-naturedly at me.

I could see that travelling with Professor Stomf would have its minor disadvantages, but these were surely a small price to pay for such an amiable and warm-hearted companion. He had now dismounted to spare his mule, and strode on ahead of me with his curious rolling gait, his chin thrust forward like the blunt prow of a ship, the blue eyes smiling under the steel-rimmed spectacles, the rubber-soled shoes splayed out as the springy turf dinted at his passing. Once he tripped over a tuft of grass, and nearly fell. 'Buda,' he cried (the name denotes a celebrated Ethiopian demon), 'Buda.' Dessime and the policemen laughed merrily. We were a contented band.

At midday we halted at a large church called Chidane Meret or the Covenant of Mercy. It was no earlier than King Menelik's time, and in consequence held no particular interest for me. But the encircling grove of junipers was delightfully cool, and I waited contentedly for the Professor to complete his examination. An hour passed; eventually he came out, beaming with pleasure at his discoveries. 'There's a painting here,' he cried, 'that shows the Crowning with Thorns, what they call the "Kouerata Resu". It's no more than fifty years old, and it's fascinating to think they were still copying or rather miscopying a Flemish picture painted in the sixteenth century and imported about that time into Ethiopia.' He showed me a photograph of a Flemish picture in which the crown of thorns was surmounted by a halo of shafts of light, mistakenly represented as nails in a modern Ethiopian copy. Though my own interest in Ethiopian paintings decreased in proportion to their youth, I found the story of the Kouerata Resu most absorbing. With acknowledgement to Professor Stomf I retail it here.

The original Flemish picture of the Christ crowned with

thorns with arms upraised must have reached Ethiopia shortly after the Moslem wars of the sixteenth century. By the time of Facilidas, at any rate, native copies had been made in manuscript and on linen. In the eighteenth century the original picture is mentioned by Bruce as being one of the most holy relics in Ethiopia. It was carried at the head of the army in battle, was said to have been painted by Saint Luke and was believed to have divine powers of intercesssion. When it was captured by the infidels at the battle of Sennaar a special embassy was dispatched for its recovery, and a vast ransom paid. Finally it was captured by the British expedition of 1868 with the other pickings from Theodore's redoubt at Magdala, and for nearly a hundred years lay in a private collection in England. About five years ago it came up for sale at a London auction-room, and this picture, that had been the most hallowed possession of countless Abyssinian kings, was bought by an American dealer for a few thousand pounds. Professor Stomf told me that it was very sad, of course, that the Ethiopian government hadn't bought it; but perhaps, one day, like the manuscript of *Alice in Wonderland*, it would be returned by a generous American collector to its rightful home.

As well as discovering a Kouerata Resu Professor Stomf had made a useful friend. The priest of Chidane Meret expressed himself touched to see a Frank so interested in Christian art, and offered all our party lunch in his tukal-hut, which was conveniently situated close to the church. It was a two-storey tukal, the first I had seen, but otherwise built in the traditional manner. On the ground floor a mule was tethered, and an old woman was pounding 'teff' in a large wooden pestle and mortar. We climbed a rough circular staircase to the upper floor, and were cordially invited in.

The priest was undoubtedly a man of some wealth, and did not spare his comfort. The tukal was furnished in what I was to recognize was a grossly extravagant manner for the country, though it was in a state of some confusion; there was a large bed, a wooden frame on which thongs were criss-crossed; under this bed was a new fibre suitcase and a piece of household crockery, beside it a Gospel of St John and a new hacksaw; various vestments cluttered the room and a storm lantern hung on the back of the door. The two most surprising single objects were a photograph of a young man in a street that I knew well in Addis Ababa, and an issue of the *Evening Standard* dated some three months earlier.

As we ate some 'wat' from an enamel dish, and drank curdled milk – I couldn't finish my glass but Professor Stomf drained his with gusto – the priest explained how the photograph had come there. His son was one of Ras Hailu's retainers; just now the Ras lived in Addis, and the photograph had been taken there.

The copy of a London evening paper was not so easily explained as the photograph. The priest mumbled something about peppermints. Dessime, our police sergeant, didn't like to ask again, but we understood that peppermints bought in Debra Tabor were often wrapped in London evening papers. I had not realized that in that abandoned town people kept up so well with world affairs.

That evening we were encamped directly below the Guna massif in a grassy plain, where numerous cattle, horses and mules were grazing. In the clear light of evening the visibility was exceptional, even for Africa. One could see a long file of animals slowly advancing from left to right, while behind them other files advanced from right to left in visual counterpoint. The plain was perhaps three miles broad. On the mountain itself there were sparse woods of juniper, and several villages whose churches were conspicuous among their wooded groves – one called Michael and, astonishingly close to the summit, one called Mariam.

We had halted at a curiously anonymous village; there was no church, and Dessime could not even elicit from the inhabitants whether it had a name. But it was an excellent place to camp. The plain was carpeted with soft grass at this point; what stones there were had been eroded by wind or rain into convenient shapes for backrests, footstools and hooks for tethering the mules by; while an unexpectedly mild wind blew down from the mountain above us. Two of our policemen quickly lit a fire from pieces of dung lying scattered about us, making a rough tripod of stones on which they put our kettle, then gingerly coaxing the flaming lumps of dung into the best positions. With the help of the third policeman I erected the patched Ghibbi tent (now on its third outing with me) and installed the camp-bed and my knapsack. One foolish omission I had made was to forget my sleeping-bag; I could picture it now padding the hard

A boy with amulets to ward off a demon called Buda. At first I was sceptical of the need for them.

mattress of my bed at Mr Rams'; fortunately the missionary had lent me a large horse-blanket which I hoped would prove to be nearly as warm. The kettle boiled at last and we sat round the fire drinking our tea and eating boiled eggs and 'injerra'.

There was no doubt that, despite our little detours and our protracted halts to observe the countryside, one could not have hoped for a more entertaining companion than Professor Stomf. As we munched our food he told me some of his adventures in the country before his arrival in Gondar. 'I took a mule to Lalibela,' he announced, grinning ruefully at the thought, 'but the poor animal was as frightened of my camera as any Moslem woman, and shied violently whenever I took photographs. Eventually I was thrown off and my thigh-bone was bruised so badly that I had to be carried for a day on a rough stretcher of poles – that's how they carry the sick in the country. At every village we came to that day, they flocked out to see who was going by. That night I found three girls would take shifts to sit beside my bed so exciting was the sight of a Frank to them.' 'How did you talk to them?' I asked. 'Oh, I couldn't speak a word of Amharic, of course, and I had no interpreter then. I was also not in the mood for conversation, being half paralysed with exhaustion and illness. But I managed to establish good relations by waggling my ears. You know it's amazing how quickly you can explain things in dumb show if you really have to.' Professor Stomf beamed at me. 'Of course that was an extreme case. I shouldn't be certain it would work every time,' he added modestly.

It was a convivial evening. Professor Stomf had insisted the policemen joined us, and had given one of them half a dollar to buy some anise in the village; later the mule driver, Ato Kiffli, had joined us, bringing his assistant. Professor Stomf was still swapping anecdotes with them when I crawled into my tent and addressed myself to sleep. Professor Stomf had gently declined my offer to share the tent, on the grounds that it would offend the policemen.

During the night I woke five times; there was a brilliant moon and it was now fiercely cold; once I put my head out of the tent and saw a meteor burst explosively above the long dorsal fin of Mount Guna. Professor Stomf, a smile on his craggy features even in sleep, snored round the embers of the fire beside the three policemen.

In Debra Tabor we had been told that we should reach Bethlehem on the evening of the second day. It soon became clear that this was too optimistic an estimate. We set off next morning in the bitter cold of dawn, and by midday had not yet crossed the boundary into Gaint. For this lackadaisical progress one particular reason suggested itself.

Professor Stomf, as I have said, believed in studying people as they were, not as we chose to make them. Further implications of this theory now began to be revealed. When the policemen decided that it was time for a drink, after a bare three hours of the march, Professor Stomf generously gave them half a dollar to buy 'talla' and rested happily under a juniper tree till they returned an hour later seriously the worse for drink; twice we lost our way for half an hour before being directed by villagers on to the right track. Equally, when our muleteer Ato Kiffli announced the mules were exhausted – this was soon after the policemen's protracted elevenses – Professor Stomf suggested we both dismounted to give our poor mules a rest. I fear I concurred with a bad grace. Professor Stomf, his injerra-bag slung jauntily over his shoulder in a parody of the Ethiopian style, strode blithely on ahead of his mule, singing a pretty song of Old Vienna. The song had a curious effect on his sense of direction; his mule, trotting faithfully behind him, reflected his zigzag course with the precision of one boat being towed behind another. I pointed out this interesting fact to Professor Stomf, who declared that he was zigzagging to avoid the mule.

Long after midday we came to a vast gorge, the frontier between Debra Tabor and Gaint. In the anfractuous chasms a brown river toiled northwards to Lasta. After a steep climb down the gorge's rocky sides we splashed across the water, easily to be forded so long after the rains, and crossed gratefully into Gaint. Soon we were in a different land – a featureless steppe, unscarred by the plough, hardly grazed by cattle or sheep. We plodded on, passing only an occasional wayfarer. By evening we had climbed to the saddle of a long ridge and the whole country lay spread out at our feet: Mount Guna, a vast brown massif behind us, tinged pink with the afterglow of evening; ahead, across the dizzy chasms of Lasta, a spiky panorama of blue mountains – here lay

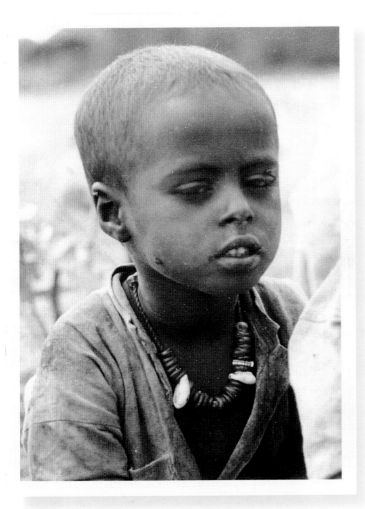

Most children in the

country, and some

even in the towns,

wear amulets round

their necks to protect

them from various

evil spirits

Lalibela three or four days' journey to the north-east – while to the south the lean ridge on which we stood dipped suddenly into a series of delectable green valleys, dotted with villages and clumps of eucalyptus; in this direction lay Bethlehem. As night fell like a velvet curtain over our view we tottered down a pebbly path into the nearest valley, the valley of Zuramba. We pitched camp, with difficulty, bought some eggs from the inhabitants who were curiously unsympathetic towards us, and settled down for a night of bitter cold.

The following day was the first day of the Tom, the great Lenten fast. We left the valley the following afternoon, the ground beyond Zuramba falling steadily and vegetation becoming more prolific. We passed several clumps of kosso trees, which it was always a delight to observe, and scattered woods of juniper. Our path down the wooded defile was again a well-trodden market-road. We repeatedly met caravans of donkeys carrying cylindrical sacks of grain; sometimes there would be a cry of '*Professore, Professore*' from Dessime and our leisurely party would be scattered by a dozen heavily-laden donkeys which came suddenly from behind, driven on by an impatient posse of drovers; at other times it was we who scattered a dilatory caravan or a herd of cows that were wandering aimlessly across our narrow path, guarded only by a ragged child with a stick.

Just before dusk we reached a village called Minchuha. It was noticeably warmer than it had been at this time the previous evening and we were now perhaps 2,000 feet lower. Once more we heard the grateful rasp of cicadas; the fields were grassier than those of the more exposed uplands; a gurramailee sang waveringly in a tall eucalyptus tree on the village green. We lit a fire from the ample supply of firewood that was stacked by the village – the policemen appropriated this as a matter of course – and our kettle was soon boiling. The villagers sold us some eggs without complaining, for which we paid the equivalent of a farthing apiece; they themselves were unable to use them because this was Lent.

About nine a full moon rose above the walls of the valley, and the headman appeared carrying a broken lemonade bottle full of anise. Like all the officials we had met he seemed pleased to see us, but this hospitable gift was exceptional. After exchanging the usual ritual of question and

At last we emerged from the woods and came to a stubble field in which three mangy-looking donkeys were gleaning the last ears of corn in company with a family of baboons. Beyond this field the path fell in rapid spirals to a village below. This was the village of Bethlehem, the large circular building its church.

answer about our route I asked the headman where he got the anise; was it distilled locally? No, it came from Coma Dinga, the village we had passed two days before. Ah, then he must be an important man to buy his drink in the next province. The headman nodded complacently. But his brother, he said after a pause, was more important still. He was a colonel in the army stationed at Harar; these ample eucalyptus trees were actually his little investment in this area. I told him that I had met his brother in Harar unless I was mistaken; was he not rather tall with a toothbrush moustache and a scar across one cheek? What a charming man he was. The headman welcomed me almost like a family friend. It was not till he had brought a second bottle of anise that I remembered that the colonel I had in mind was not in fact stationed at Harar, but in Addis.

After the headman had gone, leaving his son behind to 'entertain us', as he said, the party became merrier still. Professor Stomf was in his most puckish mood, while the policeman and Ato Kiffli were unusually expansive. Dessime gave a drunken imitation of Professor Stomf in a church: 'Kouerata Resu–Christos-Mariam–Kouerata Resu', imitating the Professor's didactic manner; while the subject of these sallies called Dessime our 'Colonello' and Ato Kiffli a 'Ras'. It was a happy evening, perhaps the happiest of our trip. Tomorrow the mysteries of Bethlehem would be unveiled, but now our thoughts were for the moment. After midnight I sank stupefied into my tent, leaving Professor Stomf still doing his celebrated jig in the moonlight to the slow hand-clap of our escort, under the astonished eyes of the untravelled villagers and mules in whose field we had so brashly set our camp.

The village of Minchuha, like many in this area, had migrated during the years since the village church had been built; the collection of tukals that made up the village was now some half an hour's journey away from the church. So when Professor Stomf suggested next morning that we make a detour to see what paintings it contained, I was far from happy. Eventually I allowed myself to be persuaded; Dessime said he believed that our path would lead by way of the church to Bethlehem.

Inside the grove of junipers was an inner ring of olives and atwat trees, the first I had seen since Belesa, while the

grassy churchyard was crowded with a merry huddle of villagers gossiping after their Sunday Mass. Professor Stomf courteously asked if we would be admitted, and some of the villagers, not waiting for the chief priest, unlocked the door and let us in. The church was unusually thick with dust and hay pollen. Under the dusty draperies were a group of rather crude early nineteenth-century paintings. The villagers began to furl the draperies with long bamboo poles, as Professor Stomf prepared his camera for photographing the Kouerata Resu. Just then I sneezed, and at that moment a very odd thing happened. To explain it I must refer to the strange Ethiopian notion of Buda.

Most children in the country, and some even in the towns, wear amulets round their necks to protect them from various evil spirits; amulets are also worn by cattle and horses. The amulets are made from pieces of cloth or skin enclosing magical incantations against spirits, written by the debtera themselves. The principal evil spirit is a demon called Buda. He can be the direct cause of a catastrophe – like sickness or a fall (hence Professor Stomf's frequent cries of 'Buda' with looks of fear and horror which never failed to divert our policemen). He can also take possession of men and even of animals.

LEFT: *The Governor of Nefas Mucha ('Place of the Winds') and escort.*
ABOVE: *The first sight of Bethlehem – and my heart sank.*

Junipers by the church wall at Bethlehem – built from cut stones like a medieval wall. Dare I hope for the best?

I had discovered most of these details in conversations with Professor Stomf; Buda came close after the Kouerata Resu as his speciality. It remained his ambition to see a Buda actually at work.

Now when I sneezed in the choking dust of the church's inner ambulatory, I disturbed from the church roof a myriad of black bats, which fell to the ground like flakes of soot all round us. Of a sudden the whole mass of villagers, including both priests and children, threw themselves on the bats; a moment before they had been frozen to the walls in attitudes of prayer; now they stamped and flailed at the bats in an orgy of destruction; some bats were even dispatched within the sanctuary of the church itself where they fled for safety. It

was a savage massacre, more macabre because it was inexplicable – unless the bats were being dispatched in the name of Buda. Professor Stomf was convinced that he heard one priest cry 'Buda', like an officer reading the Riot Act, just before the congregation set upon them. I was sceptical of this, though after the sequel to this scene I was more inclined to agree with this dramatic diagnosis.

In the churchyard the mules were curiously skittish. My own neighed pitifully when I tried to mount it. I imagined that it missed its companions, the two baggage-mules that had been sent on the direct route to Bethlehem while we made our detour to the church. Professor Stomf was having similar trouble with his mount. Eventually, after bidding good-bye to the villagers and giving them candles for the church, we trotted off by a narrow path across the shoulder of the hill which led to a bridge of rocky ground connecting this hill with the next. Though there was a sheer drop of several hundred feet to the river below, I was perfectly confident in the mule's sense of balance; we had

Eureka

traversed as precipitous paths as this before. Yet for once the mule's behaviour was rather unnerving when we reached the bridge of rocky ground. For some inexplicable reason it kept very close to the edge of the path, as though it wished to keep a close watch on the chasm. I was thankful when we reached the grassy hillside opposite, and turned to Professor Stomf to see how he fared. At that precise moment I suddenly felt myself swing upside down under the mule and fall violently to the ground. The girth had suddenly snapped, though it had seemed strong enough when I had harnessed my mule that morning.

'Buda,' cried Professor Stomf jovially. 'I told you there was a Buda in this place.'

Rubbing my hip-bone, which had been bruised by the exposure meter that I had in my pocket, and examining the exposure meter, which proved to have been broken by my hip-bone, I felt that I would not doubt the presence of the demon again – not, at any rate, while I was a hostage in his territory.

By midday we had climbed to a great plateau overlooking the country in which they said lay Bethlehem. My hopes were frequently raised by the sight in the plain below us of a grove of trees; each, however, proved to contain a circular church, and none were Bethlehem. We ate our lunch in the shade of a bamboula tree in a village where Ato Kiffli had friends. They were unable to give or sell us any injerra (or curdled milk for Professor Stomf); they declared that they had hardly enough for themselves, and despite the fertility of the area the village certainly looked poor enough. So we had to make do on tea and some withered rounds of injerra we had been given in Zuramba.

After lunch the going became more difficult as the path led down to the plain through first a forest of junipers, and then thickets of agam and cantuffa. We led the mules, stopping occasionally to ask the way; the farther we got from Zuramba the more uncertain were our guides of the route. At last we emerged from the woods and came to a stubble field in which three mangy-looking donkeys were gleaning the last ears of corn in company with a family of baboons. Beyond this field the path fell in rapid spirals to a village below. This was the village of Bethlehem, the large circular building its church.

At first I refused to believe Dessime when he showed us the village. The village church, a mile or so obliquely below us, was not significantly different from the others we had passed; it was an exceptionally large church it was true, but circular in shape with a conical roof of thatch. Surely this could not be the church we had come so far to see.

Dessime was adamant. From the directions we had received in the last village this was the valley of Bethlehem, and the only church in sight must necessarily be the church of Bethlehem. The logic of this was impossible to deny. With sinking spirits I stumbled down the stony path towards the church. I was hardly cheered by Professor Stomf's merry talk of the Kouerata Resu that might be contained within.

When we reached the village it was desolate and deserted. Priests and villagers, Dessime guessed, must be up the valley at a feast to celebrate the making of the talla. In their absence we had to decide a question on which there was a disagreement between Professor Stomf and myself. I was for pitching my tent at once in a delectable grove of junipers by the church wall; this would present the priests with a *fait accompli* should they take hardly to our presence. Professor Stomf on the other hand was in favour of a more delicate approach. 'Let us not be precipitate,' he said as we sat by a fly-blown village hut, from which an industrious line of dung-beetles were rolling their balls of dung. 'It would be discourteous if we pitched the tent unasked in so holy a spot.'

I was on the verge of an argument on this question when a group of villagers and priests came flocking back into the village. They crowded round us and questioned Dessime excitedly about our provenance and our motives for coming. Dessime replied with spirit. Professor Stomf and I were both flattered by these attentions, though we accepted the admiration of the crowd in a different way; Professor Stomf distributed peppermints to the children and amused them with his dumbcrambo act, stopping only to bow low in greeting to the elders; my cool Anglo-Saxon temperament

With the shock of an explosion the glorious truth burst upon me. The church was just as the Barambas had described it, *both* round and square: the tukal church was simply a rude veneer overlying an older church. Preserved inside the circular mud walls and under the conical roof was a rectangular medieval church...

EUREKA

allowed me no more than a series of nods. The villagers were eventually joined by an emissary of the Mamre, or high priest, who announced his master would welcome us shortly.

In the Mamre, as in a few of the priests we met in the deep country, there was something of the grave but gentle dignity of a lama. 'Welcome to Bethlehem,' he said without even asking to see our letter of introduction to him or our official laissez-passers. 'It is many years since we have seen a Frank here in this valley. May God reward you for coming here, whatever the purpose of your visit.' To this speech Professor Stomf replied with extravagant politeness, and waved a silver cross that he had bought at Axum to show that we too were Christians. He then asked courteously if I might be allowed to pitch my tent in the market-place. 'By the church wall,' I put in quickly. The Mamre consented and then withdrew, promising to send some food from his own kitchen. Soon a plentiful supply of injerra and eggs were stacked beside my tent. Later a deputation of villagers brought a second tent for Professor Stomf and the party; the tent was apparently used at Timkat.

We had now spent some time at Bethlehem, and yet I had not so much as set foot within the church wall. Perhaps I had been subtly influenced by the Stomf doctrine of restraint; though I rather think I was putting off the dismal moment of finding the church of Bethlehem no more or less interesting than the rest of Gaint's country churches.

As I approached the church, one oddly exciting detail now caught my eye. The immense circular wall of the church was built from neatly cut stones, not from the rubble of rough limestone constituting the walls of all buildings since the time of Facilidas. I did not dare let myself hope this was a good omen. Sure enough, within the church compound the worst was apparent. Below the conical roof we had seen from afar off there was a conventional fence of mud and wattle. I crept dispiritedly onwards. From the outer ambulatory of the church came the muffled boom of kettle-drums. I peered within the wattle fence. In the echoing ambulatory was a vast rectangle of stone. At centre and on either side were huge doorways of juniper wood.

With the shock of an explosion the glorious truth burst upon me. The church was just as the Barambas had described it, *both* round and square: the tukal church was simply a rude veneer overlying an older church. Preserved inside the circular mud walls and under the conical roof was a rectangular medieval church: the vast stumpy timbers of the doorways, and the pink stone walls polished like

LEFT: *the outside wall of the church of Bethlehem, clearly showing the exterior wattle fence which hid it from the outside world. The inset crosses are unique to Bethlehem.*

TOP LEFT: *Frescoes of the Annunciation – with Mary receiving the Angel Gabriel at her prie-dieu – and St George* (TOP RIGHT).

RIGHT: *'I know you will think that I'm joking,' said Professor Stomf, 'but I can tell you these graffiti are the most valuable discovery we have yet made.'*

porphyry were finer of their sort than any yet known. In the lyrical moment of the discovery I rushed forward, and knelt to kiss the doorpost of the church with more fervour than the most fanatical Christian kissing the stones of the Holy Sepulchre at Jerusalem. If I had not yet conquered the Mountain, I had at least discovered an entirely unknown medieval church.

The next day passed in a happy flurry while we examined the exterior of the church. Superimposed on the pink stones of the west façade there were numerous eighteenth-century frescoes painted on linen hangings; some were sadly battered and had been crudely restored with blue overpainting (a picture of Mary, a St George and a Crucifixion were defaced in this way); but most of the frescoes had survived intact. I had to admit that for once the effect was aesthetically most pleasing. The normally harsh colours had faded to a delightful grisaille; while the actual figure-drawing was most moving. For the first time since the discovery of the painting at Wehni, I felt that here was an artist at work, not merely a copyist content to make a pastiche of Renaissance and Byzantine art. The pleasure I took in the paintings was further increased by one painting which literally fell into my hands.

In order to examine the paintings Professor Stomf was standing precariously balanced on a kettle-drum; this in its turn was balance on an old packing-case (perhaps this had once contained the Timkat tent). Beside him, like some awful stick-insect, his plate-camera stretched its spindly tripod legs, which were equally precariously balanced on a kettle-drum. 'Kouerata Resu–Mariam–Georghis,' the Professor murmured for the benefit of the priests, and was as usual rewarded by a murmur of approbation at his learning. To me he complained sadly that the picture of the Crucifixion with its most interesting modern overpainting was so tattered that his photographs would not do it justice. 'Wait,' he added, 'I have an idea.' Professor Stomf descended gingerly from his perch, and trotted off to the tent.

Five minutes later he was back with a little envelope of powder. 'Luckily I brought some flour,' he said. 'There's no glue like flour and water.' He mixed a little into a paste , using water from a gourd in the church porch, and

remounted to his tottering seat on the kettle-drum. Soon what remained of the figure of Mary was being restored to its original position by the Cross. The priests, who had momentarily regarded the Professor's actions with suspicion, now applauded his generous restoration.

One agonizing problem, however, remained. Mary's right hand was too withered to be restored; and it hung limply down, threatening to undo all the work of restoration. Professor Stomf stood bemused on his drum pondering this problem; one hand held the restored fragments to the walls, the other the gourd of flour paste. It was a critical moment and I acted in the only possible way. I seized the withered hand of Mary; like a ripe apple it fell into my hands. There was a frisson of horror among the priests.

'I must take this to Gondar to show his Excellence, the Governor-General, how this church needs money,' I said with divine inspiration. The priests slowly recovered their smiles.

Professor Stomf had returned panting to the ground, and though he did not seem grateful for my presence of mind, he was soon distracted. Even more exciting for him than the eighteenth-century frescoes were some modern scribbles on the north wall, which, he declared, threw an entirely new light on the problem of the Kouerata Resu.

'I know you will think I'm joking,' he said, 'but I can tell you that these graffiti are the most valuable discovery we have yet made.' I assured Professor Stomf I did not think he was joking.

For me the rest of the day passed in an exultant analysis of medieval Bethlehem. The juniper wood doorways, though grander and better cut than those at Debra Damo, were constructed in the traditional way; they were in fact uncannily like the doors represented on the Axum obelisks of over a millennium before. The innovation lay in the simple rectangular plan (all other churches had indented plans, to represent the corner towers of Axumite building); in the use of massive blocks of dressed stone, fitting together so accurately that I could not but think of Egyptian building; in the adoption of a gabled façade at the east and west ends (this was surely a South Arabian feature) and finally in the curious conceit of representing crosses in the walls by inlaying blocks of whiter stone among the pink. Together these three features represented a considerable advance in the medieval style.

On the crucial question of how to reach the arcana within, Professor Stomf and I were, as was to be expected, in total disagreement. At present the Mamre was politely evasive whenever I asked permission to enter. The door remained padlocked after morning Mass. To break down the Mamre's resistance I suggested we should first offer a handsome present. If that failed we must threaten him with obstructing us contrary to the orders of the Governor-General, and if necessary the Emperor. 'You will never gain their confidence, if you do that,' Professor Stomf replied in a shocked tone of voice, adding, 'anyway it would be unforgivable to desecrate so holy a shrine by threats; better not to enter at all.'

I managed to avoid an argument on this issue as I knew my temper would betray me. Professor Stomf, I realized of course, was perfectly right that we should not bully them even if it was the best way of penetrating to the interior of the church. I was yet to be convinced, however, that in Professor Stomf's doctrine lay our best hope of entering the church.

That evening, to prepare for the rare feast that awaited us, Professor Stomf and I slipped down to the pool where the village had to go for its water. We followed the long line of village women going down to fill their water-pots. When we reached the pool of brackish water, they stood deferentially aside to let us wash before they filled their pots. I felt slight distaste at the thought that there was clearly no distinction between water for washing and water for drinking at Bethlehem; one of those water-pots would no doubt be deposited later at the door of our tent for us to drink from. Professor Stomf had no such scruples, and, stripping to his underclothes, plunged into the placid brown water with a hearty splash. The village women retreated modestly to the shelter of one of the thorn hedges.

When Professor Stomf had finished, one of them returned to watch me washing my feet. In the gentle glow of evening with the vast panorama of valley and plain thrown into shadow by the westering sun, I felt a sudden sympathy for this strange medieval village. I looked gently across at one of the village women, and she, misunderstanding the look, fled back behind the thorn hedge. A small boy stood his ground; then he came down to the pool and washed my feet, bowed low like a figure in a fresco on the wall of the church.

By the following day I realized that we had spent more than a week in the country. I decided to abandon the original plan to do a vast circuit in Gaint, making Bethlehem only the first of a series of important churches we would visit. But the problem of how to penetrate the interior now seemed, if anything, further from solution.

When I reached the tent for breakfast Professor Stomf announced cheerfully: 'I'm afraid things don't look good for us this morning. The policemen wouldn't drink their tea. That means trouble.' On my own analysis it meant nothing so melodramatic; we had all had a touch of dysentery on this expedition as was to be expected.

Professor Stomf adduced other reasons to show how our chances of entering the church were now diminished. The supplies of wat and injerra had not been replenished today; on this topic Dessime had been evasive, and it was clear to Professor Stomf that we were out of favour. 'You know, we might well be advised to come back in a week or so. The Mamre will probably be in a better mood by then.'

By evening I decided that, painful as it would be, I would have to have a show-down with Professor Stomf.

The Arcana

We sat cross-legged round a small tin of baked beans. Professor Stomf sucked an egg and pronounced it bad. The three policemen and the two muleteers gloomily munched the last of yesterday's injerra.

Our tea ration had finally expired. We drank the muddy fresh talla which tasted strongly of the grass-and-dung stopper. I was looking for a suitable opening to attack my companion – the present moment was ill-suited as Professor Stomf was generously sharing his last tin of baked beans – when we heard for the first time that day the noise of visitors outside the tent. Professor Stomf looked about him for the aspirin.

A tall deacon, with the urgent look of a special emissary, pushed open the tent flap and bowed low. 'The Mamre sends his compliments. He wishes to pay you a visit shortly.' The deacon bowed and withdrew. Two boys entered carrying injerra baskets on their heads. They were followed by a procession of boys carrying other delicacies.

Since our last meeting the Mamre looked noticeably more tired; perhaps the rigours of Lent were telling on him. But he addressed us with the same gentle gravity as before. First he said he hoped the food was to our taste. I replied diplomatically that no kitchen could compare with the

Mamre's. He then inquired if we had lacked anything in our stay at Bethlehem, to which Professor Stomf replied that far from lacking anything we had almost a surfeit of good things.

'Except for one thing,' I cut in. Despite a pained look from Professor Stomf I went on: 'It is three days since we came here, and still we have not been able to see the inside of the church.' The Mamre looked grave and mumbled something about 'ferangis'. The deacon explained things rapidly to Dessime. Soon the sad story emerged.

During the war an Italian patrol had got lost in the mountains and came to the village to ask for food and water. The priests had given them what they asked. On the third evening the officer in charge tried to break into the church. By God's providence he was foiled in his attempt, but he stole a cross from the ambulatory, and swore to come back with more men and force the door of the church. 'He never came back,' added the deacon, 'and on the third day after he had left, the cross was miraculously restored to us. Many days later the body of the officer was found dead by a shepherd.'

Before the Mamre withdrew, the deacon whispered something to Dessime who at length translated it: 'The Mamre's wife is ill. At night she cannot sleep. Can you give her something?' Professor Stomf rummaged in his pockets and produced three aspirins.

Next morning we were awakened by the same deacon. 'The Mamre's wife slept excellently. He hopes that you will be able to come and see her this morning. But first he invites you into the church.'

I ate breakfast in an agony of impatience. Then, four days after I had first seen the conical roof of Bethlehem prick up like a spire above the church wall, the padlock on the church door was at last unlocked for us, the door swung back on its wooden hinges, and we crossed the massive threshold of juniper wood into the echoing darkness beyond.

In the fleeting hour I was allowed within the church I had no time to be excited. I had too much to do with flashlight, camera and tape measure. Frantically I set about my task.

When my eyes got accustomed to the dim light filtering through the door behind me – all the windows were boarded up or so thick with dust as to be perfectly opaque – the interior crystallized into a simple, harmonious design,

sprang four great arches
which led up to a central
dome, each soffit of the
arch carved with a different
pattern. At each side of this
central dome the aisles
were roofed with a wooden
barrel vault. Beyond this, to
the east, was a second
dome over the sanctuary,
and two final bays of the
aisles, flat-roofed like the
first two pairs.

In general Bethlehem,
like the other important
surviving built-up churches,
represents a synthesis
between Byzantine and
early Christian building in
Syria and Egypt, and the
early Ethiopian or Axumite
style. The doors and
windows, the formalized
window pattern, and the
rusticated stone piers are all
heirs of Axum, while the
rectangular plan with nave
and aisles, the twin domes,
and all the details of the

though many details were intriguingly original. The nave was
divided off from the aisles by two rows of stone piers,
rusticated rather like those of a baroque church. The nave
roof was of coffered timber, while the first two bays of the
aisles had flat, low roofs with much carving and decorative
bosses of a vaguely Elizabethan character. The wooden
capitals above the piers were in the nature of brackets
supporting the roof on three sides, while on the fourth side
they projected into the nave as pure decoration to make a
sort of flying capital. Above the height of the aisles the nave
walls to north and south were decorated first with a frieze of
formalized window pattern like a triforium in a Gothic
clerestory. From the second and third piers on either side

carving on beams and arches, are heirs of Coptic Egypt, Syria
and Byzantium.

In Bethlehem, however, the synthesis has resulted in
some quite unprecedented features.

The 'clerestory' of lunette windows cannot, I
discovered, be anything but purely ornamental. At other
churches there is access by a staircase to the lofts above the
aisles which similar windows illuminate, and windows in the
exterior walls allow light to penetrate through the 'clerestory'
to the nave. But in Bethlehem there is no access to these lofts
at all, while no light can penetrate to them from outside.

The domes are also spectacularly different to their
predecessors of the medieval Ethiopian style. They are fitted

with an extraordinary sort of corbel between each wooden rib. These can only be decorative, and seem to correspond to the flying capitals of the nave. As well as being ornamental they may have had a symbolical part to play. There are eleven ribs and so eleven corbels in the central dome, the number of the eleven faithful apostles.

Last, there are the wooden barrel vaults in the third bay of the aisles on either side, unparalleled elsewhere in Ethiopia. Of all the weird features of Ethiopian medieval architecture these vaults are surely the most remarkable. Think of the process by which Roman traditions were translated to Roman Egypt and Roman Syria, hallowed by use in Christian churches, carried south across the Red Sea to distant Ethiopia, and finally adopted in an equatorial church where wood, not stone, was the favoured material. To some these wooden vaults may seem the most perverse features of an outlandish school of architecture. To me, however, they seem the most exciting feature of all.

As far as I know we were the first Europeans ever to enter the church of Bethlehem.

As a discovery, the church exceeded my wildest hopes. There are only four stone-and-wood medieval churches known in Ethiopia: Debra Damo (which I had visited), Imraha Christos, Jamadu Mariam, and Debra Libanos in Eritrea. All these have been known to Europe since the sixteenth century. Yet none of these could be called typical of the Ethiopian style then prevailing. Debra Damo was built excessively early – some time between the sixth and the tenth centuries – and is the bridge between the Axumite style and the medieval style. The later churches, Imraha and Jamadu Mariam, are both built in a cave, while Debra Libanos in Eritrea is built on a cliff ledge; these sites have stunted their designs. Only Bethlehem stands grandly in the open, like most stone-built medieval churches that Alvarez saw in the years shortly before the invasion of Mahomet Gran. It is miraculous that in Bethlehem we can see still preserved today a fine example of the typical medieval style.

The Mamre kept his word and our mission was now fulfilled. But before leaving Bethlehem, we had to complete our part of the bargain. After dinner his servant led us to the tukal where the Mamre lived with his wife and family.

The tukal was the largest in the village – almost the size of a small church – and a particularly fine example of rustic architecture. The conical roof was held up by a vast central pole; this branched out into spokes like those of an umbrella; and the lattice work of wattle and straw gave a charmingly cottage-like effect to the interior, further increased by the ropes of onions hanging from the beams of the roof. We sat on an Indian carpet next to the Mamre, while his daughter began to boil coffee for us over a tripod.

Professor Stomf began to examine the Mamre's wife. After a short examination he announced she had nothing worse than a touch of sciatica. 'Everybody does over fifty,' he cried rubbing his back and groaning histrionically. 'Look, I'm in agony myself.'

This performance elicited a wan smile from the Mamre, who asked if Professor Stomf took medicine for it. Professor Stompf produced a phial of sleeping-pills and gave it to the Mamre, adding that he could send more from Debra Tabor.

Our last sight of Bethlehem as we set out next morning was as moving as the first sight had been disappointing. We had interrupted the Mamre at his office in the church, with the news that we must be going; he had insisted he came to see us off, and all the priests and deacons laid down their drums and rattles and followed him. Now we stood at the bend in the road leading up the hill from Bethlehem making our last farewells. Behind the solemn crowd of priests the great church was silhouetted against the early morning sky. We bowed low to the Mamre and all his flock; they bowed low in return. 'Would that I could come with you to Debra Tabor. But may God go with you on your journey,' said the Mamre gravely. We thanked him courteously for all his hospitality. Then we mounted, and after a last look at the church and its priests, we started the long climb towards the hungry slopes of Mount Guna. The Mamre's son was apparently to follow us, in order to fetch the medicine for his mother.

By that evening we were back on the icy steppes. At evening on the next day we saw the sprawling mass of tukals spread out below the holy hill of Debra Tabor. Professor Stomf left the medicine at the Governor's ready to be collected. I never heard if it reached Bethlehem. Perhaps the Mamre's son missed us on the way; or perhaps his father

LEFT: *Boys waiting for Professor Stomf to distribute peppermints or explain the miracle of life in dumb show.*
RIGHT: *The valley near Zuramba where we got an inexplicably cool reception.*

I said farewell to the Professor in Gondar a day or two after our return from Debra Tabor. Just as at our first meeting, a month before, he was surrounded by a mass of curious children. He grinned at me without a thought for the past. 'Good-bye.' He waved hilariously, and was lost to view at the turn of the road.

would not allow him to leave their Shangri-La, that lost valley behind Mount Guna.

We at any rate had done our best for the Mamre. I say 'we' – in fact it was Professor Stomf, as usual, who had seen to this philanthropic act. And I find myself guilty of a worse distortion of the truth than this. When I am talking of Bethlehem – 'the only recorded example of the fully evolved medieval style, the climax of Ethiopian medieval architecture' – I catch myself speaking of our joint discovery as though I had made it single-handed. (For this there is an excellent precedent in James Bruce, who antedated the death of his companion, Signor Balugani, by nearly a year in order to claim unaided discovery of the source of the Nile.)

I said farewell to the Professor in Gondar a day or two after our return from Debra Tabor. Just as at our first meeting, a month before, he was surrounded by a mass of curious children. Today he was distributing peppermints and at the same time trying to explain the miracle of life in dumb show, assisted by the example of a cow that had just calved in a shed by the main road. When he saw me he desisted for a moment. 'Good-bye. See you in Addis Ababa,' I said rather brusquely. The memory of my own unseemly behaviour at Bethlehem still rankled. 'Good-bye.' He grinned at me without a thought for the past. 'Good-bye.' He waved hilariously, and was lost to view at the turn of the road.

From that day till this I have not met Professor Stomf. He did not reach Addis Ababa, on his way back to France, until I had left for the provinces. I have not been able to trace him in Europe. Today Professor Stomf may well be back in Ethiopia, as he often said that he would like to return if funds and health permitted: 'I haven't got long,' he would say as we huddled round our camp-fire, 'not at any rate living at this altitude – my heart's not as good as it might be – but I should like to finish my work on the Kouerata Resu before I go.' Perhaps even now he may be back in the highlands, striding across the steppes with his injerra-bag over his shoulder, crying 'Buda' when he falls. If he should read these pages – who knows, he may buy his peppermints wrapped in them – I hope that he will spare a thought for the intolerant and impatient companion who once journeyed with him to Bethlehem and nostalgically recalls today the crazy enchantment of that journey.

5 Chapter Five

Nor where Abassin Kings their issue Guard,

Mount Amara (though this by some supposed

True Paradise) under the Ethiop line

By Nilus' head, enclosed with shining Rock

A whole day's journey high ...

Milton: *Paradise Lost*

Plans for a Pilgrimage

Of the three mountains that had at one time been royal prisons I had yet to visit the second, Amba Geshen, 'the Grassy Mountain'. From Stephen Wright I gathered that there was no particular difficulty in reaching the place; it was two days' journey north-west from Dessie.

LEFT: *Buying a straw umbrella in the market near Addis. I myself bought a saddle cover emblazoned with the Lion of Judah.*

PRECEDING PAGES: *Shoan landscape with ambas. A lithograph by J. Bernatz (1841)*

He himself had passed close by on a journey from Wollo Province across to Begemdir, and he believed several travellers had visited it quite recently looking for manuscripts. Nothing, however, remained of any antiquarian interest.

After my return from Bethlehem to Gondar, and the flight back to Addis, I resolved to visit Amba Geshen. Even if nothing of historical interest remained, it was well worth visiting for its associations.

There are various stories about how Amba Geshen was chosen to succeed Debra Damo as the second mountain of the Princes. Fr. Paez, the Jesuit missionary who built the Palace of Suseneyos at Gorgora and wrote a history of the country, relates that King Yekun Amlac restored the custom by imprisoning his five sons on Geshen in 1295.

Alvarez, who reached Ethiopia a hundred years before Paez, records a different tale. God appeared in a dream and told King Abraham, the successor of King Lalibela, that he must confine all his sons on the summit of a high mountain. He gave the King two hints about the choice of a suitable successor to Debra Damo. It would be two days' journey round the base of the mountain, and they would see 'wild goats on the rocks looking as if they would plunge into the abysses below'. The King sent his men to search the kingdom for a mountain as large and as precipitous as that described by the Almighty. Eventually they reported that Amba Geshen filled both requirements, and this became the royal prison.

During the fourteenth century Amba Geshen, also known as Amba Israel, became one of the chief centres of the Kingdom. As well as a prison for the Kings' sons it became the repository of the King's treasure. Rumours of its greatness filtered through to Europe; it is probably the Amba Nagast marked on the centre of Fra Mauro's Mappamundi of

Roads passable
for motor traffic

Land over
10,000 feet

Route followed

to Asmara↑

ANGOT

Fitarawi's
Castle

Mt Abuna Joseph ▲
13,827 ft

R. Cachinaraba

LASTA

Culmust

Mbaijo

R. Shall

Lalibela

Ahun Tugre

R. Tacazze

Kossamba

Ghenetta
Mariam

DALANTA

Tamboko

Waldia

Amba Geshen

Bethlehem

REGNO DE
BIAN CAN

R. Bashilo

R. Kass-Kass

Cundi

WOLLO

Dessie

1460. The rumours were confirmed in Alvarez' account of Ethiopia published after his visit to the country in 1520–21. Alvarez could not himself visit the amba, as it was jealously guarded; however he heard many stories of the grim life led by the princes, and at Lalibela he actually met one, who had recently escaped from Geshen, being led back under arrest. Both he and his mule were covered with black hoods, in which slits were cut for the eyes, so that the escaped prince's identity would be concealed; henceforward the prince lived like the 'man in the iron mask'.

Soon after Alvarez had left the country, Mahomet Gran invaded the rich tableland of Abyssinia, and for the next decade systematically plundered the country. Amba Geshen, being the royal store-house, was one of the principal targets for attack. For a time it resisted. 'The polytheists,' as the Moslem chronicles records, 'hurled down blocks of stone wrapped in skins on the faces of our soldiers.' Eventually the Moslems overran the fortress, captured the immense store of treasure preserved there, and put both the prisoners and their guards to the sword, thus inflicting a doubly crushing blow on the hard-pressed King of Ethiopia. When the wars ended the twin churches on Geshen were rebuilt, but its days as a prison-mountain were over.

Such was Amba Geshen's role in Ethiopian history. For these associations alone I should have been happy to make the pilgrimage to visit it; but the Mountain also played a large part in European literary history which would make my visit an act of literary piety. It was the second Mountain of Rasselas. Equally it played an important role in *Paradise Lost*.

In 1613 a lyrical account of Amba Geshen, under the alias of Mount Amara, written by a certain Fr. Urreta was published in a travel anthology called *Purchas, His Pilgrimage*. He had not himself visited Ethiopia but took his account from an Ethiopian adventurer he met at Valencia – a certain John de Baltazar, who claimed direct descent from one of the Three Wise Men. But though most of Urreta's tales were soon rebutted as the wildest fantasy, the legend persisted. In due course it provoked the imagination of both Milton and Johnson, and thus grew more famous still.

There was indeed a particular reason why the legend of the prison that was a paradise should be so satisfying to the palate of Europe. Since the days of the Early Fathers, the Christian world had puzzled over the problem of the site of the Earthly Paradise. The chief clues were contained in the lines of Genesis: 'From the Garden of Eden flowed four rivers: the Tigris, the Euphrates, the Pison and the Ghion.' The Ghion, in the text of the Septuagint, 'surrounds the land of Ethiopia'. Hence a case could be made, as it was by St Bonaventure, for Ethiopia to be the site of the Earthly Paradise, on the assumption that the Ghion was the Nile; though the favourite candidate was always the land between two rivers, Mesopotamia.

When Milton wrote *Paradise Lost* he drew heavily on Purchas. Though he sited his paradise in Mesopotamia, the Abyssinan paradise was awarded an honourable mention. More than this, Milton used Purchas' description of Geshen for the description of the real paradise in Mesopotamia. He took the pillars of alabaster, the single path of ascent, and the overhanging cliffs, and made them his own; but instead of Urreta's guards, the archangel Gabriel sat at the gateway. Thus the towering massif of Geshen, incongruously Abyssinian, rose out of the level plains of Mesopotamia. No ziggurat of Babylon had ever looked like this.

Amba Geshen, alias Mount Amara, prison or paradise, unquestionably deserved a visit. I could combine it with the pilgrimage to the rock churches of Lalibela that I had long dreamt of. I arranged to leave for Dessie, the capital of Wollo province, as soon as I could. My only worry about leaving for an excursion into the country was that somehow the opportunity to master Wehni would arise and as soon dissolve again while I was absent.

The firm hope I had clung to throughout the anxious and often idiotic vicissitudes of my quest for the Mountain, was that Asserate Kassa, all powerful in his province, would one day return to Gondar. Now, four months after he had first spoken of returning, he was still so firmly rooted to his Ghibbi on the flanks of Entotto that it almost looked as if he were a prisoner. In view of his continued absence from Gondar I at last turned to another patron.

I was assured that the Crown Prince would be most interested to hear about the Mountain; I guessed that the question would be spiced for him by the thought that I had at first sought help from another quarter. Accordingly I sent some photographs of the Mountain to the Crown Prince in

Lenten Fare

We left Dessie fragrant with the Small Rains; but the place seemed no more alluring even now that we were leaving it. We trotted out past the half-completed Crown Prince's Ghibbi, and the melancholy telegraph pole that Haptu said was used for the last public execution of a shifta which had taken place a year back. My mule's unshod hooves tick-tocked on the irregular tarmac with the musical beat of a woodpecker. I felt nostalgic for Europe but happy.

To the right of us a number of tinkling streams ran obediently from the boggy fields into a culvert where they passed beneath our road and were lost to view. The motor-road, though it had carried virtually no motor-traffic since the Italians had left, was furnished with an elegant pavement and frequent bridges. Only one feature was awry; the kilometre-stones at the side of the road indicated we were taking the road to Asmara, not Gondar; Haptu explained that in the hectic moments of the retreat the Italians had reversed the kilometre-stones in order to mislead the Commonwealth troops pursuing them.

That morning before we had set out Haptu had made one change in our plans which somewhat disturbed me. He insisted on bringing along his 'brother', Asafa – he was actually no relation – to keep him company on our pilgrimage. All he asked was that I should pay for Asafa's food as well as his own; this he was sure would cost very little extra; and Asafa spoke better English than he did. At first I jibbed at the extra cost – I had less than thirty dollars left now in my money bag – but when Asafa appeared from behind the bush where he had been lying low I was soon persuaded. Like Haptu he carried a scout knapsack, a blue beret and a small headscarf on which the words 'S.I.M troop – Be Prepared' were proudly inscribed in English and Amharic. After all, I reflected, one could not have too much Baden-Powell lore in these remote places, and Asafa could help carry my extra luggage.

The sad truth was that my resolution to travel with as little luggage as possible had been shaken when I bought the teapot, and had been further undermined by a gift from the kindly Swedish doctor of some tea and sugar, and an enamel tooth-mug. I had now restated the principle as follows: anything that a rich Ethiopian of the country might be reasonably expected to possess I could add to the list of the obvious necessities like camera and European clothes and sleeping-bag that I was bringing already. I had sent Haptu out before the mule's arrival to buy these extra luxuries; an ever-ready torch from Hong Kong; a school exercise-book for my journal whose cover was decorated with a crude portrait of the Emperor's sons entitled 'Their Royal Highness Princes of Ethiopia' in English, Arabic and Amharic; finally a packet of aspirins and a small DDT bomb that I relied on to defend me from fleas.

The last gangling suburbs of Dessie were nearly past us when we met a caravan of donkeys trotting into the town with

Haptu

bags of grain bobbing on their backs. The drovers were typical country folk; the men barefooted and wearing headbands and coarse cotton knee-breeches with a short shamma like the Greek 'chlamys', thrown loosely across their shoulders. My memories of Gaint returned with a sharp pang, and I was glad to find that paradoxically I felt nostalgic for the deep country as well as for Europe. The drovers stopped when they met us and asked us without any particular show of interest where we were going. 'Geshen, Geshen,' explained Haptu. The

muleteer fixed it with a little electric-light flex. He himself must have been about thirty, and wore a small goatee beard with the assurance of a successful literary man. Haptu said that in fact he was ill-treated by his grasping old father; he was a good friend, however, of both of them; they had all worked together in the Highways Department. Now he trotted along behind the mule, with a contented look on his face, and from time to time, to show he was a good Moslem, he lit a cigarette. (Smoking is discouraged by the Christian Church of Ethiopia, as the tobacco plant supposedly thrived on the hill of Calvary.)

drovers' attention, only half occupied anyway, was now diverted by a seedy little Arab shop in this suburb; its shop window was piled high with shoddy European goods – kettles, glasses, bars of soap, mirrors, sweets, enamel bowls, razors, even cigarettes which are taboo for Christians on religious grounds. The drovers gazed wide-eyed at the luxury of this display, like children at their first tea-party, or the moonstruck Chaplin of *City Lights*. I had seen something of the sort before in the market quarter of Addis, but never witnessed the moment of impact so vividly. Poor bumpkins, I reflected, to think that they take this to be civilization. A few weeks hence I was to remember these thoughts ruefully enough.

We were now at last free from the shackles of the town. Ahead of us a trough of boggy green fields was contained between two lines of low hills. We splashed across the boggy track beside the road, with frequent pauses to adjust the loads. Haptu's knapsack came adrift, but was tied up with the scout headscarf; the girth of the mule came loose as usual – these girths of cowhide thongs inevitably did – but the

While the motor-road clung primly to the hills, our track made bold detours across the fields of young corn. These fields struck me as being a peculiarly iridescent green, the colour in fact of the fields round Winchelsea as Millais painted them in 'The Blind Girl.' I asked Haptu if the crops were a special Ethiopian variety. It turned out that it was just ordinary wheat, but the fertility of this part of the eastern escarpment was apparently renowned. If the rains came at the right times they could grow three crops a year here. To me the black loamy soil was no cause for delight, as the mule tended to skid on the slopes. I was relieved when our track left the funnel of green fields, turning westwards through a gap in the hills into a broad grassy plain, peppered with mules and sheep, cows and horses.

As usual the place seemed underpopulated; the plain could surely have supported three times the amount of livestock. Haptu loyally explained that the Government were trying to get the country people to breed more livestock.

'Look,' he said, when we came to an unusually large ram grazing close by the track, 'this is an American Point Four ram. The Government have sent it here from Addis. Now they will be able to breed better sheep here.'

The subject of our conversation, the Point Four ram, was a truly magnificent animal, barrel-chested and as shaggy as a polar bear, the kind of ram I had always imagined Ulysses used in his escape from the cave of the Cyclops. But somehow I could not believe that it was happy in its work. There was a faraway look in its eye. I have seen that look in the eyes of oil-men from Idaho drinking cola in the deserts of South Arabia; of New England tourists eating buns in Bath; it was the faraway look of the expatriate; the Point Four ram, too, pampered and cosseted as he was here, doubtless felt the bitterness of separation from his own.

After this melancholy encounter, my spirits needed reviving. But the clouds, which till now had been content to lie heavily on the low hills beside the plain, now settled on the plain itself. A steady drizzle ensued, making the going more slippery still, and the light

gaberdine of my coat and jodhpurs limp and sodden. I managed to tuck my sleeping-bag under the protection of the saddle, but the saddle as a result bellied out under me so that riding became uncomfortable. Haptu and Asafa bore the rain more stoically than I, although they were still more lightly dressed than I was, and their gym-shoes were continually being sucked off in the mud. 'We will sing you a song,' said Haptu, seeing me dispirited; 'would you like an English song or one of ours?' I asked for both. Together they sang a sad little marching song about Alabama, which they had learnt from the American scoutmaster; then they sang a love song in Amharic whose refrain went: 'If I say that I love you, why must you say no?' Now all three of us felt dispirited.

At midday our caravan was joined by a woman with an umbrella and a basket of hens on her way to a weekly market at a village ahead of us called Workaria. She proved an immediate restorative to us all. 'He'll do,' she cackled pointing to me as I hunched over my mule. 'I haven't had a man for some time.' (Haptu was very coy about this but I got the translation at last.) I looked curiously down at the woman who offered herself so readily. She was old and corpulent, and she smelled strongly, like almost all Ethiopian women but successful courtesans, of the rancid butter which is used as an unguent for the hair. I explained to Haptu as tactfully as I could that I hoped it wouldn't be rude if I declined her generous offer. He translated this, and she brandished the brown umbrella she carried, bursting into an obscene gurgle of laughter, and then began to sing a

Hyenas, from Bruce's Travels (1790).

bawdy song, pointing at me all the while with her umbrella. Haptu and Asafa laughed till they cried, shouting out occasionally, 'She means you, sir,' which was perfectly obvious to me. Further than this they would not go; eventually, after much pleading, I was allowed a bowdlerized translation. I have no means of knowing how much has been excised but I give Haptu's version here:

It's love, love, love –
My husband is a fine man and gives me money –
From other men I need no money.
But for the stranger from the far country
My belly will be ready
For love, love, love.

The rain had stopped when we halted for lunch. Beside the track, close to a pair of Moslem graveyards bright with euphorbia and aloes a rough stall had been set up to serve passing wayfarers. I had not seen a stall like this before; Haptu said that they were common enough on the caravan trail, though today being market day at Workaria, the stall would hope to do better business. We sat cross-legged on the ground, ate sweet injerra made from wheat (instead of the sourer 'teff') and drank vinegary talla from gourds; the injerra was seasoned with 'berberi' or chillies, the simplest way of eating it; the meal cost less than 30 Ethiopian cents (a shilling) for the three of us. Haptu and Asafa still felt hungry, so I ordered a second course of chick-peas and roasted ears of corn. We offered what we had left to our muleteer, who proved to be called Hassan. He declined the offer (he had brought a loaf of Italian bread wrapped in an old newspaper and was happy eating this with a little berberi) but he volunteered some information on the Moslem graveyards beside us which intrigued me, as they were so remote from any village. 'The first,' he announced gravely through the medium of Haptu, 'is for children. They will go straight to paradise and must be buried separately. The second is for thieves. They will not go to paradise, and they too must be buried separately.' This arrangement seemed fair enough, if there was ample ground to spare. But it was odd, none the less, that there were fewer graves in the children's cemetery than in the thieves'.

At dusk that evening we reached a village called Cundi in a gorge beside the River Kass-Kass. Haptu said it was the village where the pilgrims on the annual excursion to Geshen Mariam rested for the first night; so we had kept up a pilgrim's rate of progress anyhow. I asked Haptu to arrange for us to have a night's lodging along with our fellow wayfarers: a merry band of donkey-drovers, a debtera dressed in skins and carrying a fly-whisk on his way to a church far to the west, the Mamre of the large church near Geshen who kept himself apart from us, and an amiable policeman whose wife rode beside him on a bay mule.

The village headman of Cundi was already hard pressed to find accommodation for this party when Haptu gave him my message. 'Hasn't the Frank got a tent?' he asked, considerably put out. Haptu assured him I hadn't. He examined my papers and gloomily admitted that I had a right to some sort of accommodation. 'There is nowhere left,' he said at length, 'except the donkey-stalls. It will be better there than outside.'

If I had foreseen how I was to pass the night I should gladly have accepted his offer; but we dilly-dallied a bit, and in the interval Asafa rushed up excitedly with the news that he had a 'brother' here, who offered to put up all our party in his father's house. This proved to be an unusually large tin-shack but already it contained as well as the 'brother's' family most of the donkey-drovers, the deacon dressed in skins, and the amiable policeman and his wife; with the addition of our party there were twenty-five crowded into its smoky interior.

What with the heat and the noise and the exhaustion of the day's ride, I soon contracted a burning headache. They offered me a vegetable wat, but I couldn't eat anything. I took four aspirins from my store, peppered my sleeping-bag with DDT and laid it in one of the niches scooped out of the mud walls, and then despite the merry hum of conversation among the mule-drovers, the shrill cackle of our hostess, the crying of their sick child, and the lowing of oxen in the annexe of the hut, instantly I fell asleep.

When I awoke the dinner-party was in full swing; I had only slept a couple of hours. The pain that I now felt was so fierce that I found I was groaning aloud. At first I thought I had been struck down by some frightful disease. On the first day of the journey this would be too much – but gradually I realized that the pain was not more than surface-deep; in myself I felt much better. I groped about for my torch and felt the reassuring touch of its cool, chromium frame. What it showed me was not, however, reassuring at all. A trail of large termites led directly along the mud niche under my sleeping-bag and hence out of the door of the hut; despite the DDT a number of termites had evidently strayed inside. I hastily moved my sleeping-bag on to the floor, where Haptu and Asafa lay under their shammas. After a while the pain of the termite bites moderated, and merged with the familiar bites of fleas, with which the mud floor was thickly populated. Haptu and Asafa were scratching and tossing about under their assault. For me, after the pain of the termites, the flea's bite was but a caress.

When I awoke again, the noise of the dinner-party had subsided to a gentle murmur. Soon, however, there was a bang on the corrugated iron door of the shack and Hassan and six more guests appeared. Haptu whispered to me – we were all fully awake by now – that they were fellow Moslems whom Hassan had found in the village. 'They have to eat now because of Ramadhan,' said Haptu as they began to bang and clatter about the hut, waking everyone up with convivial shouts. Our host rose sleepily to his feet and his wife began to cook a second wat, using meat as well as vegetables.

It appeared that the Moslem fast was significantly different from the Christian Tom or Lenten Fast. We had to fast from midnight to midday; during the rest of the day we had to abstain from all animal products, including milk, butter, eggs, meat, etc. Moslems, on the other hand, practised no special abstinence whatsoever during Ramadhan; but their hours of fasting were more trying than our hours; neither food nor drink must touch their lips from dawn to dusk. In consequence strict Moslems would have to take their meals, like workers on a night shift, at intervals during the hours of darkness. This explained the late arrival of the new guests – though hardly Hassan's behaviour.

During the day he was not a strict Moslem; he had eaten an excellent lunch. But now in the hours of darkness he was tucking in like the most fanatical believer.

The Moslem dinner-party lasted an hour or two, and we had peace and a blessed interval of repose till a cock began crowing hoarsely for a premature dawn. The call was taken up by the other cocks in the village. One even flew up on to the tin roof above our heads and flapped its wings with a weird metallic noise. There were still some hours before daylight, but as Haptu and Asafa were now wakeful like myself and Hassan had not properly gone to bed, I suggested that we should leave Cundi, provided we would not give our hosts offence. Haptu seemed to think he was used to guests who left early, so we collected our baggage together and stole from the shack. We found Hassan had hobbled the mule behind a clump of trees. It was quickly saddled, and in the coppery glow of a late moon we splashed through the river Kass-Kass and clattered out along the stony caravan trail to the west.

The Earthly Paradise

it was a Rock
Of Alabaster piled up to the Clouds,
Conspicuous far, winding with one
    ascent
Accessible from Earth, one entrance
    high;
The rest was craggie cliff, that
    overhung
Still as it rose, impossible to climb.
Betwixt these rockie Pillars Gabriel
    sat
Chief of the Angelic guard.

Milton: Paradise Lost

Every year for five years Mahomet Gran invaded the Christian Empire of Ethiopia during the great Lenten Fast or Tom; he reckoned that the severity of the Tom would have weakened his enemies' resistance.

This severity I now began to feel for myself. The sun rose rapidly behind us; after we had crossed the Kass-Kass and its affluent the Talayil, the heat became oppressive; soon we left the stony track that a ploughman told us was the road to Geshen; in the sun's heat and with the exertion of climbing I became exceedingly thirsty. But according to the rules of the Tom I was not allowed even a sip of water till midday. The drinking-horn, which I had bought in Addis and filled from the Swedish doctor's tap, was leaking steadily; to see the water dripping needlessly away made my lips drier still. And now that we were climbing steadily we passed ever more frequently mountain streams splashing across our path. Haptu and Asafa, to my surprise and irritation, seemed quite unaffected by drought.

At eleven o'clock I could bear it no longer.

I dismounted and made an equivocal gesture which suggested to my party that I wished to relieve myself. When they were safely out of sight, I drank greedily from one of the cool cascades pouring off a neighbouring rock. Feeling that I

had behaved rather shabbily, I rejoined the others. Ten minutes later I observed Haptu drop behind and snatch a drink from a stream while he thought my back was turned; probably they had both been doing this the whole morning. From now onwards it was the accepted but unspoken convention amongst us that we could at least drink before midday, even if eating was forbidden; but we never gave scandal by drinking in full view of the others.

One of the reasons why Geshen has attained such fame in Ethiopia is a legend that here the True Cross was buried by St Helena after she had rescued it from the infidels. This legend is held to be supported by the shape of the mountain; the rock is cut in the shape of a cross. (Haptu confessed to me that he rather thought the mountain had shaped the legend.) From here, however, none of the five ambas looked

at all cruciform. I rode to the nearest village to ask the way, with the rest of the party tagging wearily on behind.

The village headman or shum invited us to his hut with a great show of courtesy, and to our delight revealed that Geshen was the first amba in sight; it was no more than an hour's ride; the churches on the summit were concealed by the thick grove of gum trees. This was excellent. The shum suggested that first we had lunch with him. I thanked him cordially for the invitation; I had not eaten for twenty-four hours and I did not conceal the fact. 'Why do you not eat?' he asked rather sadly. 'You are ill like my wife?' 'Yesterday I was; but today I have not eaten because of the Tom.' The shum expressed himself amazed. 'He is a Christian too,' he said to all the assembled company who were equally struck by this

marvel. I revealed the silver cross I had bought at Axum – a trick I had learnt from Professor Stomf. There was a fresh outburst of applause. To show his esteem for me, the shum told his daughter to cook the best vegetarian wat they could provide. While she was boiling up a paste of beans and onions and berberi, the shum asked me anxiously if I could do anything for his wife, who had severe pains in her stomach, and one of his children who had something stuck in its throat. 'Look,' he said eloquently. The child was brought in, held upside down, and shaken violently like a bottle of mixture. 'There is something stuck there, and it will not come out.'

It was a melancholy fact that the deeper we got into the country, the more sickness and disease we saw. With my

THE EARTHLY PARADISE

pitifully small store of aspirins and lack of medical knowledge there was little I could do; the only comfort I could give was to commend the sick people I met to the excellent Swedish doctor in Dessie with whom I had been staying. To the shum of this village I now gave this rather unhelpful advice. He thanked me, but I saw he wasn't considering their going. He was perfectly philosophical about his sick relations; the child was brought in a second time and shaken as before. 'Perhaps it will come out tomorrow,' he said, 'there is certainly something stuck there.'

After the wat, eaten with sweet injerra, and handed to each of us individually in order of precedence (I noticed that Hassan, either as a Moslem or a muleteer, came last), the shum excused himself. He was off to Dessie to take some bags of grain to the weekly market. Haptu and Asafa asked him to take with him as well some letters for their friends in Dessie; it was apparently accepted practice in the countryside for market-goers to deliver mail in the absence of any postal services. The shum agreed and Haptu and Asafa industriously scribbled notes of the 'Just arrived. Having a wonderful time' sort on two pages of my exercise book. They blushed when I asked them to whom these tender messages were addressed, and I guessed, correctly it proved, that they were writing to

their girlfriends. I had, alas, no girlfriend within a thousand miles, so I had to be content to write a bread-and-butter letter to the hospitable Swedish doctor. Entrusted to the care of the shum it would reach my late host (though forty miles of trackless mountains now stood between us) considerably sooner than most bread-and-butter letters I wrote in Europe – or so I imagined. Inexplicably it never arrived at all.

Alvarez speaks of the ascent of Geshen being so steep that cows, mules and goats had to be dragged up with thongs. To us, as we approached the amba, the ascent looked remarkably tame.

In the few miles we had traversed since the shum's hut the mountain had assumed the cruciform shape it was supposed to have; from each arm of the cross the ground fell in flaking terraces of rock and grass and shale; at the eastern arm of the cross which sprang directly from our plateau, a broad staircase was cut in the rock up which I could see, like spirits ascending to Paradise, a caravan of mules and donkeys lightly ascending.

An hour after we had left the shum we reached the foot of the eastern arm and began the ascent ourselves. I suppose that in all the amba rose 1,000 feet above the plateau, itself some 9,000 or 10,000 feet above sea-level, but the tiers of

I had stumbled on a new discovery: an unrecorded fifteenth-century Book of Gospels showing (LEFT) *the Presentation in the Temple,* (RIGHT) *the Raising of Lazarus.*

rock, formed by each new stratum we came to, provided frequent respites from the climb. With no particular effort we passed the several stages and reached the foot of the staircase. Here Hassan suggested we left him and the mule. There was a village near by where he could stay, and find fodder for the mule; no doubt as a Moslem he had no wish to go higher up the slopes of the holy mountain. Already we could see the huts on the summit fringed with prickly pear and with machicolated wooden struts overhanging the abyss. We unloaded the bedding and continued up the staircase. At the seven hundred and third step – I could not resist counting them – we reached the doorway which in Milton's verses would have held the Gates of Paradise.

The gates were made of corrugated iron. A tired old sabanya, remote from the Gabriel of *Paradise Lost*, sat between the two mud pillars of the doorway on a battered wooden stool. We showed him our papers; a messenger was sent to fetch the monastic guest-master, who soon hurried up; the barbed wire which hung like rusty briars about the doorway was roughly pushed aside and the

iron gates rattled open.

From the amba's summit we could peer down into the vast, vertiginous abyss below. The evening sunshine picked out the gunmetal coils of the river Talayil we had forded that morning just before we started the ascent. Paradise or not, it was true that the mountain was 'a whole day's journey high'.

The monastic buildings were not a romantic sight; a medley of huts sprawled across the summit of the amba among a grove of blue gum trees. Among them an occasional turbaned monk flitted past bent on his devotions; there were even a few withered nuns. I was glad when our guide showed us the guest-house. It was a large tukal in the centre of the amba, carpeted with a thick Indian carpet, clean and reserved only for us. We dropped our luggage and set out to explore the amba. A crowd of boy deacons – much better dressed than those of Bethlehem or Debra Damo – formed the inevitable escort on our tour.

In Addis Ababa and the provincial capitals, the most important churches are built in a style that I find totally uninteresting: they are built of stone and roofed with tin,

(LEFT) *the Holy Family, and* (RIGHT) *Christ with the signs of the four Evangelists.*

materials which together dictate an octagonal rather than a circular plan; in other respects they are as uninspired in design as the mud and thatch churches of the country, and lack their rustic charm; these octagonal churches are usually the work of Italians. In Amba Geshen we found that the famous churches of God the Father and Mariam had lately been reconstructed in this modern idiom. This was an unwelcome surprise. I knew from Almeida that the medieval churches had been destroyed by Gran. But I had not expected that anything so rich and modern would now have replaced them in this remote spot; these were the first tin-roofed churches we had seen since Dessie.

Beside the shiny church of Mariam was something even more modern still – a heavy stone plinth surmounted by an outside umbrella cast in bronze and illuminated by fairy lights lit by a small generator beside it. It was apparently a sort of ceremonial stand for the Ark on processional days. I had never seen anything like it, and the monastic guest-master assured me that it was not yet a year old. I paid a hypocritical tribute to its charms. 'Ah,' the monk exclaimed

eloquently, 'if you knew what trouble we had getting it here from Dessie – and the price we had to pay. But no other church has got one like it – not even Georghis in Addis Ababa.' I agreed with him that not even Addis could rival him in this. If truth be told, I was beginning to wonder why we had left that stately city at all if this was the deep country.

However, when we walked past the shiny new churches, and the glittering bronze umbrella, I did find one interesting relic; a deacon sat astride the shattered head of a stone column which had the characteristic Axumite design cut on its capital. It was surprising to find it so well looked after, and I asked the monk why they had not thrown away this dirty old column. 'Ah,' he said, 'this is sacred. St Helena left it here to mark the spot where she had buried the cross on which Christos died for us.' We talked of the finding of the cross. I was told that King Zara Yacob and St Helena had flown with it to Geshen, flying by way of Mecca. (Like so many Ethiopian legends the story had obviously been derived from an Arabic original; small price to pay for this was a detour to Mecca.) I thanked the guest-master. He flitted away to his office; I believe a sort of Vespers was taking place. Haptu and I strolled on to the end of the southern arm of the cross, where we halted solemnly once more to peer into the stupendous melancholy void.

From the Mountain of Wehni the prisoners had looked down on a valley as lush and Arcadian as any of a poet's imagination. From Debra Damo the prisoners had enjoyed a moderately fine prospect of valley and hill. The situation of Geshen was more melancholy than words can describe. How ironical that Milton should have chosen Geshen to be his Earthly Paradise.

Later that evening in the hospitable darkness of the guest-hut, we discussed our journey to Lalibela with the kindly guest-master. He confessed that he had never been there himself, but believed that it was possible. 'How many days' journey?' we asked anxiously. The guest-master went off to inquire. 'Two days,' was the reply he brought back. 'Tomorrow we will show you the way.' The guest-master had also brought back a special gift from the Abbot's own kitchen – a tin of Victoria plums. This was the compensation for the modernity of Amba Geshen, and my romantic bias for the past did not deter me from taking more than my fair share, before I curled up on the Indian carpet lining the floor and fell into a grateful sleep in which I dreamt that, like Ruskin at his first sight of the Alps, I saw ahead of me on the horizon the walls of a lost Eden.

In the crisp morning sunshine the monks seemed different people from the muted, bat-like creatures of the evening before. When I looked out of our hut-door to see about a bowl of water for washing, a party of young deacons went tripping past the door with happy, half-term cries; an older monk, no less cheerful, trotted past carrying a large missal. I was surprised to see such levity in Lent. Soon the Abbot's servant appeared with a bowl of water. When I had washed in this I asked Haptu where I should go to accommodate myself in no less important manner. Haptu translated this somehow, and the Mamre's servant pointed to a party of deacons tripping past the door; apparently I was to follow them. I tagged on to the last of them, and after several hundred yards of serpentine paths among the huts we emerged into the open. This I thought would never do; to my relief our party soon passed once more behind a screen

of gum trees and quickly reached the edge of the amba.

On our way up the staircase we had observed the curious way in which the framework of the huts overhang the abyss like a sort of machicolation. I had presumed that this was some sort of fortification; I now saw otherwise. It was the monastery privies, that were corbelled out, in this practical way, over the empty void. (Later I found there were parallel arrangements for the nuns on the other side of the amba.) The monks ahead of me now accommodated themselves in a line, most of them talking and chattering with unusual animation, while a few read their psalters. I approached my place with a certain diffidence; there was a sheer drop of several hundred feet to an unsavoury precipice below. But the structure looked pretty strong, and was firmly dowelled into the rock; I took my place.

Back in the guest-hut I explained the arrangements to Haptu and Asafa who laughed irreverently. For myself I believe that, apart from the shattered stone column, this was the only relic of medieval Geshen; the idea is too ingenious and too clean to be more modern; like the monks of medieval Europe those of medieval Ethiopia were pioneers in the field of hygiene.

Till now the Abbot of Geshen had not appeared, but had acted through the medium of his personal servant and the guest-master. The reason for this was that the local bishop, Abuna Michael, was on a visit here. After the morning office had finished, the Abuna sent his servant to tell us to pay a call on him. We found him resting on St Helena's stone, a weary old man, with face of a Christ by Peiro della Francesca, surrounded by a group of attentive deacons, dappled by the early morning sunshine which filtered through the gum trees. I bowed low, and he nodded to me in a fatherly way.

The conversation which ensued was polite and unexceptional. Where were we going? Did I live in Addis Ababa? Had I enjoyed my visit? There was, however, one difference I noticed between these questions and those of my previous journeys. The Mamre did not ask my motive for coming; he accepted my pilgrimage as a compliment to Geshen that was no less welcome because it was expected. Before we parted he volunteered the news that there were old manuscripts in the church; he was sure that as a Frank I

was interested in such things. I thanked him cordially and he hobbled off, supported under either arm by two young deacons. It was clearly no light task to make a diocesan tour in this province.

The talk of manuscripts did not, to be frank, thrill me. The exciting medieval ones were so rare – perhaps no more than a dozen illuminated ones in good condition are known altogether – that the search for them had proved too heartbreaking. The post-medieval ones had now lost their appeal for me. At Geshen I knew there were neither; a traveller had recently visited Geshen to look for manuscripts, and found nothing of interest. Out of mere politeness I now asked to be shown those of the church's manuscripts which were illuminated.

To my surprise I was taken to the actual store-house where the manuscripts were kept; always before the manuscripts had been brought to me. The store-house was a leaky annexe of the church of Abba, crammed to bursting point with new and old missals and prayer-books, whose texts were painted on vellum and bound between wooden boards. I rooted about for some time without finding anything of interest, and was just about to give up when I caught sight of a red-boarded Book of Gospels of an unusually large size. It was covered in a wrapper of modern chintz. Negligently I opened it.

To my amazement I saw that it was illuminated in the best fifteenth-century style. I had stumbled on an unrecorded medieval manuscript which proved to have no less than thirty-six separate illuminated pages. When my excitement had moderated, I studied the find carefully.

The force and the originality of the artist were remarkable. There was a special vitality in such scenes as the Annunciation with Mary spinning and the Angel Gabriel saluting her. There were also many charming details which other medieval manuscripts lacked – the stone before the tomb a vast megalith dwarfing the four centurions, the Magi holding out their gifts like buns, and the shepherds pointing to a dream of the Nativity floating over their fields like a runaway balloon. All the pictures were miraculously well preserved; in the sunlight outside the hut they shone with the brilliant translucent colours of Chinese lacquerwork.

After I had recorded all the pictures on film, the manuscript was replaced in the leaky store-house, I should have dearly liked to study it longer. Indeed I bitterly regretted not being able to buy it from the priests. But the grand days of travel, when men like Robert Curzon bought manuscripts from monasteries in the Levant for the price of a drink, have gone for ever.

It was high time to leave Geshen. A dizzy panorama of

valleys, above which we were exposed like offerings on an altar, faced us on three sides; across the deepest canyons lay our path to Lalibela. If we travelled all day I reckoned we might be able to cross this low country and reach the plateau which emerged again twenty miles or so beyond. To spend the night in the abyss would be to invite the attentions of malarial mosquitoes. There was also a chance of meeting the shiftas who, people whispered at Dessie, operated in the land between the rivers below us. In all soberness I believed no more in shiftas than I did in the demon Buda; I had noticed both were being manipulated by people to dissuade us from visiting certain places; but I was not

brash enough to put my scepticism to the test.

We had paid our respects to the monks, left an offering of five dollars to the church, and were just approaching the iron gates where the tired old Gabriel sat on his battered stool, when I became conscious that a melancholy man in a coarse grey blanket was asking for baksheesh. Though I was by now quite impervious to such demands, I was surprised to find a healthy man so importunate, and in such a holy place. 'Tell him that we are poor pilgrims,' I told Haptu. Then my curiosity got the better of me. 'Why does he want it: he is healthy enough. Can he not work?' 'He is wanted by the Government,' Haptu replied. 'He has taken sanctuary here till there is an amnesty.' Though he had now no rifle and no ammunition he was apparently a shifta.

I was most intrigued to meet one of these shadowy

Villages among the ambas to the west of Amba Geshen

figures at last. I gave him a handsome present – I am ashamed to say, nearly half of the amount that I had given to the monks. Then I began to ask him all the questions that had so long puzzled me. Why had he taken up this hazardous profession? Were its rewards compensatingly large? I even thought of asking him if he would scribble me a laissez-passer in case I met any of his colleagues. The shifta remained morose and dumb. Finally I asked him if he was going to buy more ammunition with the baksheesh I had given him. A ghost of a smile crossed his melancholy face. I have often since wondered if this man, for whom Geshen was both a refuge and a prison, made good his escape with the help of my largesse and resumed his chosen career that the Government's action had rudely interrupted.

6
Chapter Six

Then God sent an angel to carry King Lalibela to heaven and God showed him the churches made from a single rock. The number of the churches were ten and each of separate pattern and architecture.

From an Ethiopian manuscript in the British Museum

One More River

Together with Gaint and Belesa, Dalanta is one of the least visited regions of all the highlands. I had heard of no European traveller who had wandered there since the war; the Italians, judging from the silence of the Italian *Guida* and the ignorance of the Italian maps, had kept well to the south. Perhaps no European had passed this way since the days when Napier's army fought its way southwards to subdue Theodore at Magdala, perhaps no European since Alvarez.

In all we were to spend four days wandering across the cool mountains of Dalanta. Though physically more exhausting than any I had yet experienced on my travels, I felt a strange elation; this was the pilgrimage of my imagination; without guide or escort, we crossed great plains and forded great rivers; each night we rested in the hut of a local chieftain who made his home our own. We lost our way and found it once again.

How to recapture more than a shadow of those dreamlike Dalanta days?

WEDNESDAY EVENING AT TAMBOKO

Above us the last few hundred feet of the escarpment, a rocky wall with a green gateway to let us into Dalanta. The priest of the church of Mariam here promised to show us the path in the morning. He is a gentle old man, talks sadly of the days when he lived at Dessie; now he is so poor he can't repair his roof. But he brings us a gourd of honey for dinner from his hut.

We are sleeping in the church porch set among a grove of olives. The candelabra euphorbia forms a stockade all round that should keep out the hyenas. It is cool and mossy here – grateful after the heat and dust of the day. We have forded three rivers, come twenty miles perhaps. Geshen is still in sight among the misty mountains to the east.

After dinner four old men crowd round our hut.

No one has ever seen a camera before; many men of this village have never seen a motor-car. We are like divinities to them. We talk of Addis and its machines. They cannot understand what I mean by a telephone. Later we talk of Jerusalem and finally of the stars. They are astonished to hear we have names for them.

I am woken during the night by a rock-fall above us, which frightens a family of baboons. They scream shrilly.

THURSDAY. NEAR KOSSAMBA. LUNCH-TIME

Apparently it has been raining in this part of Dalanta for a month. The ground is black, boggy, brown like the underside of a horse-mushroom. They say that they are very behind with the ploughing; mules as well as oxen have to be yoked up. For us it is very difficult going. Even on this narrow watershed there are streams everywhere; to east and west they have grown into rivers; in a few miles a splashing mountain stream can grow into a river too deep and strong to be forded.

NO NEARER KOSSAMBA. TEA-TIME

The country bleaker again, rather reminds me of Montenegro; outcrops of white stone everywhere. We have forded our fifth large river today, the Gizeh. Several miles to the west I can see other caravan trails than ours converging on a stone-built bridge of three handsome spans – the only bridge away from the motor-road I know of. It was apparently built during the last century by Ras Obie. It is a moving sight to see something permanent built by man in all this rocky desolation. The new fields here have stones set up on their ends like obelisks to give more room for the plough.

KOSSAMBA. EVENING

Underfoot crocuses and violets and lobelia set in emerald fields. We passed one valley in which mushrooms grew as thickly as daisies in Oxfordshire. I picked some for supper, to the alarm of Haptu and Asafa who did not know they are edible. The shum was equally alarmed when I offered to add them to our wat.

BELOW: *Peasants going to market near Lalibela.*
They knew the way. We wandered in circles.
PRECEDING PAGES: *A dream or a miracle? The*
thirteenth-century church of Abba Libanos at
Lalibela carved out of solid pink tufa.

ONE MORE RIVER

Eventually I am persuaded that the wat is better made in the traditional fashion.

FRIDAY

Lost. All day we have wandered in a roughly north-westerly direction, though there is no sun to guide us, and I have lost my compass. Once more the whole gamut between fertility and bleakness. We will halt at the next village.

SATURDAY. KOSSAMBA. MORNING

Incredibly enough, we made a circle yesterday! We had hardly advanced five miles by the end of the day. The shum apologized deeply for not lending us a guide. Today he will lend us his son to lead us to Culmust. In a way I am glad to have another opportunity of seeing Kossamba. Today the mist has cleared from the high ground around this village; we have a dreamlike view across the tableland in which the knolls around us rise like islands above the sea of

mist; they are the colour of a Chinese landscape painted on silk, except for the great peaks on the horizon, Mount Abuna Josef and the rest; these are a fierce frosty blue and glitter as though they are made of spun glass.

SATURDAY AFTERNOON: ON THE NORTH FACE OF DALANTA

The shum's son left us soon after we started, 'to go and pray in the church.' We were lost again for an hour or two but had the good fortune to meet a woman going to a funeral at Culmust. She led us for three hours, hopping agilely from bolder to boulder; eventually she became impatient; she would be late for the funeral; we followed more slowly and here we were at last looking down on the great valley of the Tacazze which leads to Lalibela. Tonight they think we shall be there. In a way I shall be sorry. These last few days, I feel, have been happier than any on my travels.

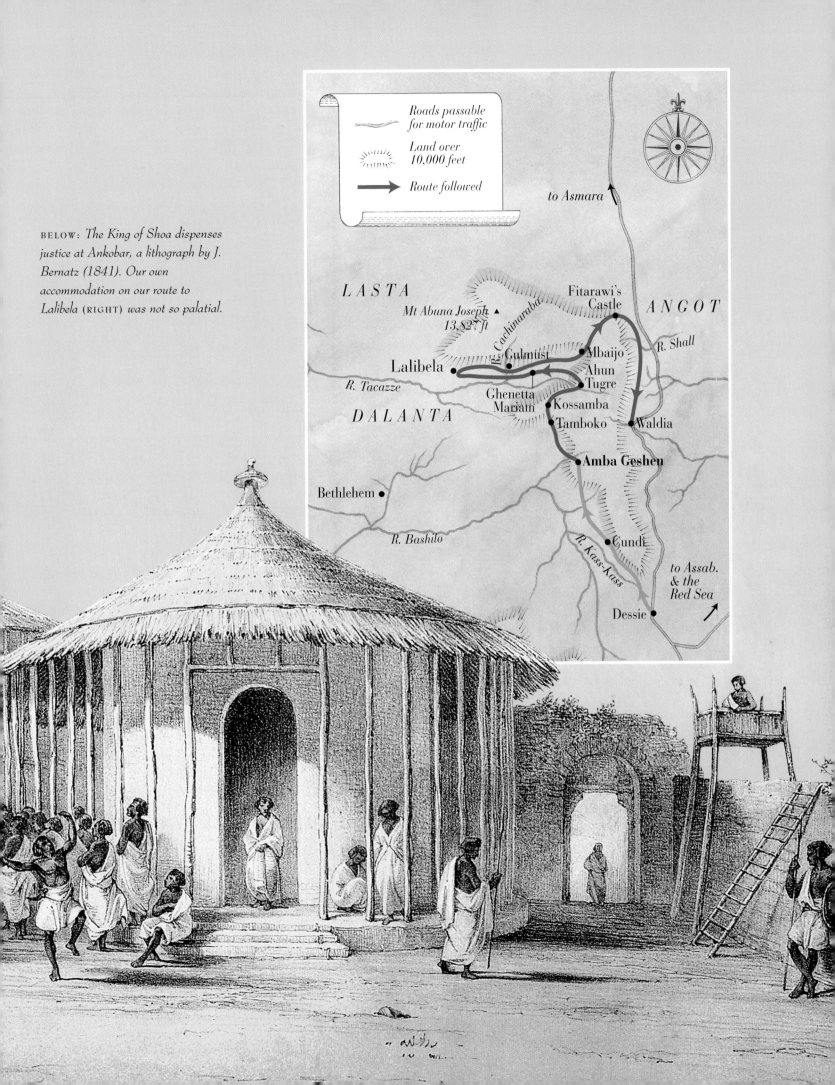

BELOW: *The King of Shoa dispenses justice at Ankobar, a lithograph by J. Bernatz (1841). Our own accommodation on our route to Lalibela (RIGHT) was not so palatial.*

Roads passable
for motor traffic

Land over
10,000 feet

Route followed

to Asmara

LASTA

Mt Abuna Joseph
13,827 ft

R. Cachinarabo

Fitarawi's
Castle

ANGOT

R. Shall

Gulmust

Albaijo

Lalibela

Ahun
Tugre

R. Tacazze

Ghenetta
Mariam

Kossamba

DALANTA

Tamboko

Waldia

Amba Geshen

Bethlehem

R. Bashilo

R. Kass-Kass

Cundi

to Assab.
& the
Red Sea

Dessie

RIGHT AND BELOW: *The rock church of Genetta Mariam - 'Garden of Mary'. I was exhausted, so we halted in a dell of wild olives. At dawn we pressed on to Lalibela.*

A few hours from Lalibela, a short detour from the dusty caravan-trail along the valley, is a village called Genetta Mariam, meaning Garden of Mary. After the day's journey, during most of which I had walked in order to spare the mule, I was very tired. Genetta Mariam seemed a garden indeed. The fields of wheat and lucerne were watered with rills splashing down from the hills above; about the fields were dotted clumps of euphorbias and weeping pepper-trees; among the conical huts of the village, in a dell hung with wild olives, gleamed the pink peristyle of a rock church. It was about five in the evening. We decided not to go on to Lalibela as we had planned, but to pass the night at Genetta Mariam.

The shum and the elders met us at the path leading up to the village, and welcomed us to their homes, in a grave but hospitable manner. Asafa and Haptu went off to prepare our beds in a two-storey tukal. While they were away the light faded over the Tacazze valley, dyeing the great cliffs between us and Dalanta indigo as they merged with the encroaching darkness. I sank into a green field at the foot of the village, which I shared with a solitary cow and two haycocks and a row of eucalyptus trees, tall and regularly spaced like poplars in the Dordogne. It was warm and dewy and the cicadas, silent for a week, began to sing in the dusk, singing ever louder as the light faded and the stars came out.

By the time Haptu and Asafa returned I was too tired

and too contented to leave my field. The villagers, though at first surprised at my intention of sleeping out, respected my wishes at length. They brought me food and drink and set them down beside me in the grass, then retired after many low bows and good wishes. I drank the talla, but gave most of the wat to the solitary cow, then lay down beside the two haycocks, and the jar of talla, and the bowl of wat, which to my chagrin the fastidious cow had hardly touched. Before the impatient tropical night closed over Genetta Mariam I was asleep.

It was the monthly feast of Mary next morning, which coincided with the last Sunday of Lent, called in Ethiopia the Hosanna. Though I should have been happy to see the feast at Genetta Mariam I felt sure that on this doubly important feast day, the dancing and the processions, the Ark and the kettle-drums should surely be enjoyed at Lalibela itself. Accordingly I roused Haptu and Asafa just when the sky flushed with the first dawn light. We loaded up the mules and were off before the first shadow of Dalanta slanted across the valley.

Back on the caravan trail, jogging along among the usual company of priests and donkey-drovers and market women, I noticed that a number of them wore chaplets of palm across their foreheads; presumably they were Hosanna palms. Haptu explained that these were pilgrims on their way to Lalibela for the celebration of Holy Week. It was fitting that we should arrive in such company. Haptu, as usual, boasted to them that I too had kept the Fast, by which they were, as usual, impressed; one old priest even came forward and handed me his palm chaplet. 'Now I feel I am going to Jerusalem,' I said as I thanked him. He looked gravely up at me. 'Yes,' he said, 'this city we call Jerusalem, so it is fitting that you should ride there with a palm for the Hosanna.' As we spoke, the city, if city it can be called, burst into view beyond the red ramparts of the valley we had been following.

The moment was unexpectedly dramatic. Robert Curzon, who travelled in the Levant in the early nineteenth century, describes the moment when their party saw the first sight of the walls of Jerusalem. He and his fellow Englishmen betrayed no emotions as they rode towards the Holy City; but the Greeks and Armenians of the party fired their pistols ecstatically and spurred on their horses into a gallop.

For us the roles were reversed. When we saw the long line of mud walls and thatch roofs ahead of us, brown and sere against the red volcanic rock of the valley, and the shimmering pool of wild olives, our fellow pilgrims appeared unmoved. Haptu and I, on the other hand, let out a wild cry of delight. We felt like the Greeks of Xenophon's army after their long march to the sea. Though what we saw was not so very wonderful – the view was remarkable only for the absence of any churches – we realized that we had come to the end of our wandering; here we could rest till the great feast of Farsiga or Easter; then with the Fast forgotten we could set out on the swift and easy journey up the valley back to the motor-road.

But we had not arrived yet; one ritual was still uncompleted. A few hundred yards before the gate of Lalibela the track was crossed by a small stream gushing from the rock. The grave priest, who had given me his chaplet of palm, stopped to drink. I thought this was very odd; the Tom did not allow us to drink before midday; it was for a priest to set an example. Haptu explained that this was no ordinary stream; it was believed to flow directly from the other city of Jerusalem; hence its name, the Yordanos or Jordan. Grateful for this indulgence we drank thirstily from the sweet water. I felt no need to observe that Axum and Debra Libanos in Shoa both claimed the Jordan as well; how fitting that pilgrims should arrive refreshed at these holy places even in the Tom.

When we were all ready we trotted up the last hill to Lalibela. The town was nearly deserted. It was nine o'clock in the morning and the townspeople, as I had expected, were still at church: we threw down our burdens under the nearest olive tree, and, led by a small child, took the dusty path to the church of Bieta Mariam. As we drew near, the familiar boom of kettle-drums and the chink of rattles were carried to our ears, but the noise sounded entirely different here. This, too, was as I had expected. With quickening steps we hurried down the path to the church below.

Lalibela

Description of Lalibela by Francisco Alvarez,
chaplain of the Portugese Embassy of 1520–26

The rock churches of Lalibela are as different from ordinary
buildings as ice is from water. They do, however, bear a
certain family resemblance to the temples of Petra – particularly as they are cut from the same sort of rose-red (or
more correctly tomato-coloured) tufa. How to explain the
weird excitement of these architectural freaks? Monolithic,
subterranean – the right flavour lies in none of these words.

This, at any rate, is the sight we saw on the morning of
the monthly Feast of Mariam, as we breasted the ridge by the
church of Bieta Mariam. Even now, nearly five centuries after
Alvarez, the first European who described Lalibela, my
journal reads like a traveller's tale.

All that is at first apparent is a rough circle of people
several hundred feet in circumference. They stand frozen in
attitudes of prayer above a large chasm in the pink tufaceous
rock. As we approach, the chasm deepens to reveal the
gabled roof of a church couched below. The chasm is
perhaps forty or fifty feet deep, and peering down between
the lines of worshippers we observe that the walls of the
church are carved with the strange patterns of windows.
Between the church and the walls of rock surrounding it
is a narrow courtyard or trench which is packed with
worshippers. From the courtyard float up the muffled echoes
of the kettle-drum.

Haptu cannot grasp how the church can have got here.
Did it sink during an earthquake? he asks wildly. I explain at
length that the church has been hewn from soft pink tufa just
as a piece of sculpture is cut away from its matrix. Haptu is
slowly convinced.

A second marvel. While we watch two priests emerge
from a porchway cut in the west façade of the church. The
windows and doors cut in the walls cannot then be merely
decorative; the church is hollow inside; hewn from the living
rock like the exterior. Inside and out the church is a
fossilized imitation of a conventional church of the twelfth
century built in stone and wood. I explain this painfully to

Haptu who is incredulous. 'Lalibela means miracle in
Amharic,' he replies, 'but I didn't expect this.'

We climb down the steps into the courtyard. Now the
circle of worshippers stands on the pink cliffs above us, their
loosely hanging shammas forming stagnant pools of shadow;
while other worshippers, contained between the narrow
walls of the trench, throng round the Ark and the drums. The
procession circles the church three times as the drums beat
and the rattles clink and the Ark is held high by the priest
under its purple veil.

Seizing the opportunity Haptu and I peer into the
church. It is very dark and white woolly veils, like those at
Bethlehem and Debra Damo, hang down like creepers from
each column. In the light of my torch I can see the gleam of
frescoes above them – in still vivid colours, an Annunciation,
and a Visitation, surrounded with the swirling designs of
cross and foliage pattern, the Solomonic star, the sun and
the moon.

Back in the fierce sunshine of the courtyard, among
patterns of cross and swastika, a lichen-hung arcade is cut in

the tufa. In this arcade there are ten columns which they say represent the ten churches of Lalibela, each column being miraculously cut as each church was finished. Leaving the courtyard, Haptu and I set out to explore the other nine churches. Five of them prove to be connected to this narrow courtyard by a maze of underground tunnels like the catacombs of Imperial Rome.

Medanie Alem (Saviour of the World), Mascal (The Cross), Michael and Denaghel (the Virgin), each are carved in extravagantly different styles.

Medanie Alem is immense by Ethiopian standards; there is a forest of columns within, each carved to represent a stone pier surmounted with a wooden capital. The church of Michael is smaller and rather sinister. King Lalibela, who gave his name to the town he ordered to be built, is buried in a vault in the church of Michael. To mark his tomb is a rough bas-relief of the King and his guardian saint. The tufa has a greenish tinge here that gives an eerie underwater

ABOVE: *Excavating the rock churches of Lalibela. From an eighteenth-century manuscript in the British Museum.* BELOW: *A fiery sermon to pilgrims at Lalibela, in 1998, photographed on my last visit.*

light to the scene. Mascal and Denaghel are hardly more than chapels opening off the courtyard of Bieta Mariam. We sat peacefully in their soft darkness while the noise of the service outside filtered in through the windows cut in the rock.

Unhappily the tunnels leading beneath the Jordan across to the other five churches – Gabriel, Abba Libanos, Mercurios, Amanuel and Georghis – are now completely blocked. We plodded across a ploughed field, tinged with the same cast of red as the rock, to the cavern where lies the entrance to the church of Gabriel. The tufa is green and slimy, making the artificial cavern like a Gothic grotto in some eighteenth-century English park. The church of Gabriel is reached by a wooden bridge – a shattered tree-trunk laid across the moat-like trench around the church. Inside it is cruder and eerie in a different way from the rest; the dim reddish light tinging an old monk who sat by the window reciting his office with a singsong voice; this old monk with parched skin and ragged dress might have been the stuffed hermit of a grotto.

Amanuel is different again from all the others, perhaps with Bieta Mariam the most appealing of all the ten. It is deeper sunk than most – we descended along a tunnel of underground steps to reach it from the shambling grottoes of Mercurios – and is more elaborately carved. Almost all the features that are to be found in built-up churches like Debra Damo are here fossilized, and a number of new features introduced. I recognized the well-known 'clerestory' and the formalized window pattern, as well as the triple row of windows, the double row of bracket capitals and the lofty barrel-vault over the nave, that are quite unknown in built-up churches. With lingering steps we at last climbed from the courtyard of Amanuel into the sunlight once again.

Strangest of all is the church of Georghis (St George). The other nine churches are rectangular and in many aspects closely resemble built-up churches. Georghis is cut in the shape of a Greek cross, and strikes out in a new direction altogether. Its window are ogival in shape with weird low-relief arabesques above; it cruciform interior is roofed with three domes giving it a Byzantine look. I took a peep at Georghis and then fled back into the sunlight; in this church the style had run amok.

Our tour complete we returned to the courtyard of Bieta Mariam, where the service was over. The priests greeted us cordially and led us to the local school. Here we installed our mule and our baggage, and ate a celebration meal of beans and talla, then slept for the rest of the day on the benches of the deserted form-room.

During the next few days we returned often to the churches, Haptu and Asafa to say their prayers; I to look at the architecture.

The churches date from the thirteenth century. But why did King Lalibela decide to have them cut from the rock in this extraordinary way? Most priests gave me the traditional reply that God had ordered Lalibela to; one, however, produced the ingenious explanation that the rock churches were designed for defence; they certainly proved invulnerable to the assaults of Mahomet Gran. One authority

*Swirling medieval frescoes on the
arches of Bieta Mariam, seen by
the light of my flashbulb.*

on Ethiopian medieval architecture believes that King
Lalibela decided to perpetuate the greatest churches of
Ethopia by having a petrified museum of architecture; this
would explain why the styles are so extravagantly different;
and almost all the features of the built-up churches can be
identified at one or other of the churches at Lalibela.

In our school compound on a ridge above the town,
wat and jars of talla were filled and emptied with satisfying
frequency. We lived a leisurely life after the exhausting days
of the pilgrimage. Sometimes we would go and dine with the
priest who was now temporary Mamre. The last Mamre had
died of what sounded to me like peritonitis the week before
our arrival, and his successor had not yet been appointed.
At other times the two young schoolmasters who were
friends of Haptu's from Dessie would dine with us in the
form-room. After meals we would play volley-ball on the
school compound.

The two schoolmasters were an interesting study in

opposites. The senior schoolmaster, who cannot
have been much more than twenty-one, had
received no education at all till he was thirteen,
beyond learning to read from the village priests,
like all Ethiopian children. He had to work as a
shoe-black in Dessie. By then, however, he had
scraped up enough money to pay for his living
expenses while he attended primary and
secondary school. He applied himself with such
zeal that he had soon caught up with his own age
group. At eighteen he won a scholarship to one
of the half-dozen secondary schools at Addis.
After a year there he had been chosen for the
Teachers Training College, and here he was, a
trained teacher at Lalibela. But the year's
progress had brought him only bitterness and
frustration. Too many young secondary
schoolboys, he said, were chasing after too few
jobs. He had been one of the relatively lucky
ones; yet here he was marooned in the country,
with no post office, no dressing-station, no
electric light, within three days' journey. 'If you
knew how much I hated the place,' he said
bitterly one night in his little den in the school
building whose bleak walls were decorated with the official
portrait of the Emperor and a nostalgic photograph of the
boulevards of Addis Ababa.

The other schoolmaster was rather older, perhaps
twenty-five. He wore an eremetical costume of skins; and
apparently would often spend the night in prayer like the
most fanatical cenobite. He came from a rich family in Dessie,
Haptu said, and had been offered excellent jobs but he had
chosen to be a schoolmaster in this remote spot because of
the holiness of the place. To me his piety seemed to find odd
ways of expressing itself. I noticed that during our games of
volleyball he would fall to his knees and would pray for
victory in a loud voice. I was assured, however, his piety was
real enough, and it was thought that he would soon be
ordained as a monk.

If I had been enthusiastic about the churches of Lalibela
I must hasten to say that in one way the place was far from
idyllic. The boy deacons of Lalibela were as fiercely attentive

Haptu cannot grasp how the church can have got here. 'Did it sink during an earthquake?' he asks wildly.

The thirteenth-century church of Georghis (St George) at Lalibela, which is carved inside and out in the form of a cross.

All that is at first apparent is a rough circle of people several hundred feet in circumference. They stand frozen in attitudes of prayer above a large chasm in the pink tufaceous rock. As we approach the chasm deepens to reveal the gabled roof of a church couched below. The chasm is perhaps forty or fifty feet deep, and peering down between the lines of worshippers we observe that the walls of the church are carved with the strange patterns of windows. Between the church and the walls of rock surrounding it is a narrow courtyard or trench packed with worshippers. From the courtyard float up the muffled echoes of the kettle-drum.

as hunting dogs. It was revealing to observe how differently they behaved from the boy deacons of Bethlehem. To those enlightened boys we had been near divinities; when we entered the church precincts they had washed our feet in the pool; with excited cries they would compete to have the honour of emptying our bowl of washing-up water; for at Bethlehem we were the first Europeans they had ever seen. Here at Lalibela they had seen perhaps four parties of European travellers a year; these were sufficient for us to be accorded the same honours as the tourists who are rash enough to land at Port Said. 'Baksheesh, baksheesh' cried the boy deacons of Lalibela, pursuing us in a dense pack from the schoolhouse down to the churches. 'Candy,' cried others in a hoarse antiphon. (The benevolent traveller who taught them this cry was surely the American I heard came this way six months before.) I had thought myself impervious to such cries, but by Wednesday I found I had heard my fill of them.

Though I should have liked to end the fast at Lalibela, I now decided against this. I had, at any rate, accomplished most of what I had set out to do, while both Haptu and Asafa were eager to be back in time to spend Easter with their families. We decided to leave at midday on the first stage of our return to Waldia, the nearest town on the motor-road.

After the five days' halt we all felt refreshed. I was glad to see that the mule too looked in better fettle. It had been increasingly feeble for the journey across Dalanta; sometimes I had had to walk more than I could ride. We loaded up after a last peep at my two favourite churches, Bieta Mariam and Amanuel, and made our farewells to the temporary Mamre. Still pursued by the importunate boy deacons we clattered out of Lalibela. We crossed the Jordan and the cries of 'Baksheesh' and 'Candy' echoed faintly across the water; soon they were lost behind.

We heard only the regular hoof-beats of the mule, the shuffling of our feet on the stony track, and the sharp crack of a whip from a field beside the road where two oxen were pulling a wooden plough jerkily across the stony ground.

RIGHT AND ABOVE: *Axum-style facade of Imraha Christos, the celebrated medieval church built in a cave near Lalibela. But the church at Bethlehem was more typical of the medieval style.*

LALIBELA

The Long Walk

Alice felt she would never be able to
talk again, she was getting so much
out of breath: and still the Queen
cried 'Faster, Faster!' and dragged
her along. 'Are we nearly there?'
Alice managed to pant out at last.
    'Nearly there!' the Queen
repeated. 'Why, we passed it ten
minutes ago!'

Lewis Carroll: *Alice Through the Looking Glass*

That evening, just before sunset, we reached Culmust, the first stage of our journey, and the only town on the caravan route to Waldia. I was tired and anxious.

Soon after we had left Lalibela the mule had begun to behave very oddly. At the slightest gradient it would stop in its tracks and have to be led; on the flat it could only manage a slow walk and blew through its nostrils hoarsely. 'What's wrong?' I asked Hassan anxiously. 'Nothing.' It walked on. When we reached the river Cachinababa, Hassan announced that the mule would be all right if we rested a while. 'But it's rested nearly a week.' Hassan mumbled something and unsaddled it. When the wooden framework was off I noticed that the spine of the wretched animal was covered in sores; to some extent all the mules I had ridden had suffered from sores, but this was the worst case I had seen; the sores were deep and gangrenous and an evil smell rose from the steaming back of the animal. 'Then it's ill, Hassan,' I said, trying to control my irritation. I wished we had known this earlier. '*Niente, niente,*' he returned sullenly, 'nothing wrong.' We rested for half an hour under a bamboula tree and then crossed the Cachinababa. The river was easier to ford than a week ago; the water was dropping fast, as the Little Rains were now finished; the grey stones at the water's edge were dyed black with the high watermark of a few hours before. It was hot, but I felt strong and well: what did it matter anyway if I had to walk for the rest of the day?

An hour later the mule stopped on a perfectly flat piece of ground. 'It is tired again,' said Hassan. 'Let us rest.' My impatience returned with a rush. It was bad enough if the mule I had hired could not carry me when I felt like riding. Intolerable if the beast could not even keep up with us. 'You

say that it's not ill,' I cried, beginning to lose my temper and shouting directly at Hassan in Italian. 'Then if it's not ill, it's just not eaten enough. By Haile Selassie, you're starving it, you brute.' Seizing the bridle of the wretched animal I dragged it a few paces up the path. The effort exhausted me; I sank down on a stone and waited for the others to come up.

Hassan, however, did not catch us up. He sat where we had left him eyeing me malevolently. My words had stung him more than I had guessed they would. Haptu and Asafa looked reproachfully at me. 'This is bad, sir,' said Haptu. 'You have insulted him.'

The imprecation of 'Haile Selassie' was a weapon of nuclear power that I had never dared to employ up till now. Though I regretted such abusive words, in principle I felt I was right to feel injured. Hassan had tried to hide the beast's illness, and now looked like delaying our return while we waited for it to recover. I had another good reason for feeling aggrieved. Contrary to the terms agreed in Dessie, Hassan had extorted from me a levy of a dollar a day to pay for the mule's upkeep and his own. This levy had drained my resources to such an extent that if the mule was now seriously ill I could not afford to hire another; on the other hand if it was merely weak from hunger, Hassan had misspent the extra money. Together these grievances had sparked off my outburst.

Hassan still sat sullenly by the roadside. Very well, I would call his bluff. I still owed him some six of the thirty dollars agreed for the trip. 'Haptu,' I cried, 'I will go on to Culmust. You two follow as quickly as you can. Leave Hassan to the hyenas.' I stalked off alone along the dusty trail. Soon the little caravan dropped far behind, the absurd red saddle-cover on which was emblazoned a Lion of Judah – a curiosity I had bought in the great Addis market – still conspicuous long after the rest of the caravan had faded into the haze.

Two hours later I reached the mighty river Tacazze which flows across half the highlands of Ethiopia, and eventually reaches the Sudan under the name of the Atbara. Here it was about a hundred feet wide. I stripped off my clothes and bathed my exhausted limbs in the cold rushing water. A passing caravan of salt-merchants were shocked to see me – shocked as much by the fact that I was washing as by the fact that I was naked; in the country

I never saw an Ethiopian wash more than his feet.

From the Tacazze it was no more than an hour's journey to Culmust, but I felt increasingly footsore. The caravans that passed gave me a wide berth; perhaps there was a wild look in my eye; it was not every day they saw a Frank in flowing Ethiopian dress (I wore my jitterbub that day for protection against the sun) striding along the trail without baggage or escort, fifty miles from the motor-road.

In Culmust I found a sad band of exiles who entertained me most hospitably; they were schoolmasters. We sat in the form-room over their vegetable wat and talla till midnight. Perversely I still kept the fast like they.

My fury over Hassan's behaviour had moderated to a nagging anxiety about the rear guard. Haptu and Asafa had not arrived by nightfall; they had all my worldly goods with them; I had to spend the night wrapped in a shamma of the senior schoolmaster's.

I was awakened soon after dawn by their arrival in Culmust. The wretched mule had collapsed altogether shortly after I had had the scene with Hassan. It was unquestionably very ill indeed. There was nothing for it but to wait in Culmust till it recovered, or to walk the two days' journey over the mountains to Waldia. In view of the indefiniteness of the delay and the necessity of starting back to Addis within the next few days for the last attempt on the Mountain, I decided to press on without the mule. I sent back Haptu and Asafa with instructions to collect the sleeping-bag and other baggage; two boys would accompany them and help carry the luggage. I only hoped Hassan would surrender them on being given the last six dollars he was owed. If all went well they would catch me up at Mbaijo, the last village before the mountains. I set out soon after they had left. The broad valley of the Tacazze was dewy and inviting; I felt strong and well after the night in the form-room; with a lengthening stride I strode towards the mountains and soon overtook a caravan ahead of me, consisting of a shum and his wife riding mules, while their family retainers trotted behind.

The Tacazze valley, which had seemed so inviting when I set out, proved to be scored with affluents on the side the path followed so that the going was never easy; the path rose and fell at regular intervals, each rise bringing the same prospect of hill and valley ahead. After two hours' walking in the sun on an empty stomach, I felt I had covered a day's march already. After three hours I wondered whether I would reach Mbaijo by midday; it might be better to stop for good at an earlier village, but none were in sight, and there was no Haptu to ask where lay the closest village to my route.

I am troubled by these anxious thoughts when a merry voice from behind hails me in Italian. It must be the caravan that I overtook earlier this morning; at its head trots an old man in a topee, a blue overcoat and carrying a furled umbrella still enclosed in its sheath of cellophane. He must be some sort of retainer of the grand couple behind me – the man wearing a sort of balaclava helmet, a rough shamma and breeches, while his lady wife, veiled with her shamma like the mourning Athena, was riding on a white mule and carrying a blue parasol.

'Buon giorno, signor,' cries the major-domo, 'bel paese qui, eh?'

Pleased to have such sympathetic company, I am soon telling him about my pilgrimage to Lalibela, the rigours of the Tom, and the ordeal I am now facing owing to the mule's breakdown. The major-domo listens attentively, then questions me about London. 'Are there roads as broad as Addis Ababa's, and motor-bikes too? Do you eat much spaghetti?' After a while his mistress who is riding behind him hears our chatter, and begins to question him about me. 'How old is he? Is he married? His parents are both dead? It is very sad.' In question and answer the words fly over his head and back again. After replying three times that I am unmarried and my parents are both as far as I know still alive, the same questions still come. 'His wife dead? How very sad. I still have two daughters alive.' I become disheartened and relapse into silence. 'Stancato?' says the major-domo. 'No,' I say fiercely. 'No. I'm not tired.' The interrogation begins again. 'What is his second wife's name? Was she married before? Has he had many wives? He is young still. But both his parents dead. It is very sad.' For the sixth time I explain that my parents are alive, that I am unmarried. The major-domo appears to explain this. Half an hour passes. 'What are his children called? They are not surely all dead like his wife and his parents? How sad.' 'Stancato,' adds the major-domo. 'Stancato, signor?' I am too exhausted to reply.

Another hour passes. I feel weaker still. Mbaijo,

Ploughing with two oxen:
photographed near Lalibela and
lithographed by J. Bernatz (1841).

excellent Mbaijo, always half an hour ahead of us, has received like a mirage. If only the caravan would leave me. I could sit in the shade for Haptu to catch up; perhaps I would even find a village near the road where I could get food. The two mules have gone on ahead, but the old man stays with me. '*Forza*,' he cries. 'Mbaijo *mangeria*.' My feet are badly blistered. I tell him feebly to go on without me. At last I am left alone. Nearby is a stream. I can drink anyway now. It is long after midday. I sink exhausted down beside the road and am almost too tired to drink.

Six hours after leaving Culmust, I tottered into Mbaijo to find that the nobleman in the balaclava, who was a Fitarawi and Governor of the Angot district, and his wife the Woizero, had together invited me to the official lunch given them in the principal hut of the village. After a delicious wat, washed down with a flask of arak, the agony of the morning seemed merely absurd. If I had not been so brashly fasting I should have surely arrived there long ago.

A new problem had arisen. The shum had apparently invited me to stay the next night in his hut in the mountains – the old man calls it a '*castello*' – and I wondered what to do. It would have been disastrous to lose Haptu and Asafa. The shum told me to leave a note, and wrote instructions of how to reach his castle on a leaf of exercise book. I left it with our host in Mbaijo. We set out as soon as lunch was over.

Our path now left the Tacazze and wound steeply upwards though a pass in the mountains among fields of barley and meadows watered with splashy streams. These mountains were cool and green like the Jura. I felt pleasantly homesick for Europe.

Our little caravan had been joined by two merchants on their way to Waldia. The kindly major-domo persuaded one to give me a ride on his horse. For most of the afternoon I jogged along on this spindly nag; it was so thin that I felt in constant danger of falling off. When the merchant left us – there is a short cut to Waldia to the south – I fell into line

again behind the major-domo. First rode the Fitarawi, than his lady wife, her parasol held high, though the sun was now invisible; then the two of us; behind us the Woizero's maid whom we had picked up at Mbaijo, together with the cook who led a large brown he-goat destined for the Easter banquet. As we went, the cook plucked ears of green barley from the fields and rubbed them in her hands to a paste; with this refreshing cordial the major-domo and I were sustained till at length we reached the Fitarawi's hut. Soon after we arrived the velvety darkness fell over Angot.

To my great relief Haptu and Asafa had found the note and followed close on our trail. We spent that night in the Fitarawi's castle. It was as grand as the major-domo had suggested. The walls were of mud and stone with two vast beams supporting an oval roof of thatch; beyond the stone wall was a stockade of wattle to keep hyenas at a distance; inside the hut, the living-room took up most of the space as usual, but there were two small rooms attached, one for the

Fitarawi's mule and the other for the Woizero's maid. This was a luxury unknown in the houses of Dalanta.

The evening meal was also a surprise. As well as the usual wat we were treated to spaghetti served on tin plates; after dinner we had coffee sweetened with sugar. I wished I had something to give the Fitarawi in return for such lavish hospitality, but unfortunately I had nothing left by now except for a small flask of whisky that I had been keeping for emergencies. I offered it to our hosts and they received it courteously. 'I am sorry we have no soda here,' said the Fitarawi with a wry smile. I explained that after dinner it could be drunk without water.

It was a convivial evening, that ended only when our hosts withdrew into an alcove where there was a large double-bed made of wood and thongs. Haptu and I settled down on a carpet by the fire, while a servant rolled a boulder across the doorway to keep out the hyenas. After the whisky I slept deeply, woke once to hear the mule neighing in the darkness, then slept again, exhausted after the events of that Ethiopian Maundy Thursday that had begun so penitentially and ended in such undreamed-of luxury.

When we abandoned the mule Haptu had secured two boys to help carry the baggage. Apparently one was a deacon of Lalibela who had abandoned his vocation for a state education in Dessie, where he had relations; the other was a boy going to Worra Illu. The two of them had carried the heavy injerra-bags, in which my bric-à-brac was stowed, all the way from Genetta Mariam, and promised to carry them today to Waldia. Their fee for this service was that I should provide their food and lodging; this had so far cost me nothing; the Fitarawi had treated them as my retainers, and accommodated them along with his own. I was much struck by such noble hospitality; Haptu assured me that this was nothing unusual for a country Fitarawi.

Today was Good Friday according to the Ethiopian calendar, the most solemn day of the Tom. I was surprised to find that before we set off the Fitarawi's wife pressed us to break our fast. 'You are allowed "gulbarn" today,' she said holding out a sticky yellow porridge of wheat and beans. I took the bowl gratefully. I was given 'moogira' too – a sort of cake rather like the barn-brac eaten in Ireland. These were apparently reserved for Good Friday alone. I explained that in Europe we ate buns on this day on which crosses had been cut to mark Our Lord's Passion. The news was most impressive to them. When I had eaten as much as I could which was not overmuch (the 'gulbarn' was as heavy as dough: the moogira as hard as balsa-wood) the two delicacies were offered to Haptu and Asafa. Wasn't the

... here a thousand are said to have sat at table when Menelik gave the ceremonial raw-meat feast at Easter to end the Lenten fast.

Fitarawi eating any? The Fitarawi said he would have some shortly. We rose to our feet. It was time for a farewell.

I felt a strange melancholy as I now said good-bye to the Fitarawi and the Woizero. Of all our hosts they had been most open-handed in their hospitality; yet I had not come to them with my letter of introduction from the Director-General; they had found me wandering and taken me in. I realized how pitifully inadequate were my thanks in return for this. I wished I had had some splendid guest-present to give them. But I had nothing valuable with me but my camera and that I could not part with. 'Would they like me to take their photograph?' I asked Haptu, anxious to do something. The Fitarawi replied, 'It is most kind of you but

The ceremonial banquet of raw meat given his warriors by King Sahle of Shoa. From a lithograph by J. Bernatz (1841). I ended my own Lenten fast in much the same way.

When Waldia was finally in sight – a mere mile away across the valley, my strength gave out altogether. I sank down in the shade of a spiky green kinchib bush and felt the numbing shock of exhaustion roll over me like a wave crashing on a surf-rider. Eventually I gathered strength enough to totter after the boy from Worra Illu into Waldia.

Less than three weeks before we had left Dessie, and on the outskirts of the town we had passed a caravan staring wide-eyed at the cheap European goods of a shanty-shop. 'Poor bumpkins,' I had

we are old now, and my wife is in mourning for her daughter. Photographs are for the young.' And so I gave the Woizero the tawdry piece of Woolworth's jewellery and said farewell. 'May God's blessing be on your head and bring you safely back to your parents,' said the Woizero. 'Good luck go with you across land and sea,' said the Fitarawi. They saw us off from the mouth of the hut. They still stood there as we walked away across the electric green fields of barley, down towards the valley of the Shall, beyond which lay the tin roofs of Waldia, only four hours' march below us.

Like all such estimates those four hours proved elastic. It was nearly dark when we staggered into Waldia, after nine hours' solid walking from Angot. We had eaten nothing since the 'gulbarn' and were a pitiful sight. Haptu and Asafa had swollen lips – they had refused to drink from the rivers we were passing saying they were too muddy – myself wild-eyed with exhaustion, and the boy from Worra Illu suffering from cruelly blistered feet. For the last three hours I had only survived by making him lead our little file; I confess it made me less exhausted to see him limping along before me.

thought at the time. Now I saw the shanties of Waldia through their very eyes. The rusty tin-roofs along the main street seemed more delightful to look on than I can imagine the burnished domes of the Kremlin seem to a traveller from the Steppes. The profusion of goods in the shops burst upon us. Coloured wool-like necklaces of jasper and terebinth; safety-pins like the silver clasps for the toga of an emperor; ingots of Lifebuoy soap heaped up in piles like the spoils of a conqueror's triumph; we gazed at these in childlike wonderment. It was like a dream of plenty in an oriental paradise. So far do a few weeks in the country take one.

That night we toasted our journey in tej served at one of the echoing saloons of Waldia. We felt like the companions of Xenophon's *Katabasis*.

Three days later, after an Easter banquet with the bank manager in Dessie where I broke both my fast and my digestion for good – we ate sides of quivering raw meat according to the time-honoured custom – I found myself once more in Addis.

The Summit

It was an Abyssinian maid
And on a dulcimer she played
Singing of Mount Abora.

Coleridge: *Kubla Khan*

During my wanderings in Ethiopia I often thought of the line from Kubla Khan about the Abyssinian maid. What did she sing about Mount Abora? Did it have anything to do with the Mountain? The story of the unattainable paradise of Mount Abora sounded as if it were in the tradition of Milton and Johnson, and I wondered if Coleridge used them as his sources. In Addis Ababa, however, I had little chance of doing any literary research, and the matter slipped from my mind.

When I returned from my Lenten pilgrimage in Lasta I found one postcard among my mail which renewed all my thoughts on the matter and filled me with excitement. It was written by a genial scholar whom I had met in Jerusalem where he was writing a book on Herod the Great. The postscript read: 'How's that Abyssinian maid? I suppose you know that Coleridge wrote "Mount Amara" in the first draft of the manuscript. I saw it once in a Paris exhibition.' This was a rare stroke of luck. With perfect propriety Coleridge, as well as Johnson and Milton, were to be associated with the three Mountains of the Princes. Reinvigorated, I threw myself once more into the intrigues which would lead me to the summit of Mount Wehni.

Ann was brimming with news about the Crown Prince. He was certainly backing our helicopter scheme. But I had reached Addis only just in time; a week later and the helicopter would have slipped through our hands. It was now assembled. Tomorrow afternoon it would have its inaugural flight before the Emperor.

But once again disaster came. The helicopter, just within our grasp, eluded us by dashing itself to the ground; the rotor had apparently been assembled upside down. This meant we must abandon all idea of using the machine. It would be months before the spare parts arrived from America, and anyway by then the rainy season would have made flying impossible. Hopes again languished.

One last chance, however, remained. Colonel Shifferaw of Gondar had once promised to lend me a sort of commando force to help scale Wehni, a plan which fell

The Mountain from the air.

'Like to fly over in a real aeroplane?' said the pilot of the Dakota. 'I'm not landing, mind you.'

through because of the Tom; 'You can't ask men to climb mountains if they're living on beans,' he had said. With the last of my dollars I flew north to Gondar to talk with him.

It proved to be in every sense a flying visit. Colonel Shifferaw gave me an excellent lunch and broke the news to me that he was posted elsewhere; he was probably off to America next month. I was just in time to return by the same aeroplane I had taken that morning from Addis.

The pilot stood drinking Coca-Cola beside me in the little tin hut on the airstrip. I told him the wretched tale of hopes raised and as soon disappointed, and he listened sympathetically. 'How far away do you say this Mountain of yours is, son?' he said, buying me a Coca-Cola. 'Three days east of Gondar by mule, that's about fifty miles. Why?' 'Well, you say you've tried to borrow a helicopter. Like to fly over in a real aeroplane? I'm not landing, mind you.' He grinned. And so over a Coca-Cola in a tin hut, the third and final expedition to Wehni was arranged.

In the belly of the silver Dakota there was that morning a typical mixed cargo of passengers: two representatives of the World Bank on a flying tour of the provinces and their guide, a young Ethiopian Vice-Minister who had been up at Harvard; an elderly country governor in the usual Burberry and topee with his two white-cloaked retainers; the wife of the Danish missionary at Debra Tabor who had been shopping in Gondar. The passengers sat on aluminium seats clipped to the floor, hugger-mugger with which were an assortment of bales and baskets and light machinery, most of it on its way to Addis. When the aeroplane lunged forward at take-off, its engines straining violently, some of the cargo slid gently backward towards the tail but returned again as the plane levelled off. The passengers sat grimly in their seats.

Soon we were 11,000 feet up in the air, aiming east, instead of taking our scheduled course south-east across the Tana littoral. We could see the brown road below, winding across the plain. After a minute or two the pilot sent for me. 'These maps don't mark any Mount Wehni. Do you think you can direct us to the place?' I squashed into the corner behind the co-pilot, and watched the Belesa tableland rise to meet us. Mount Merodo, its gateway, where we had camped; the familiar sugar-loaf swept towards our starboard wing and we gained the tableland. Michael Debra, with its vast church and

junipers; how I remembered being stranded there. The plane swept on a mere 500 feet above it. The Happy Valley at last, and the Mountain. Even the sang-froid of the pilot was shaken. From this angle it seemed more perpendicular than ever. 'Do you really mean people were stuck on the top?' he exclaimed almost incredulously. 'Boy, what a goddam place to spend your life!' Now we reached the Mountain and the plane's wing dipped as we circled it. The church, the two forts, and the grassy walls I had seen from below were clearly seen. Of a 'great house' nothing was visible. The aeroplanes's shadow swung crazily across the valley, like the shadow that a moth, dazzled by a candle-flame, casts in a darkened room.

In the months that had passed since I had first set eyes on the Mountain I had tried to picture the life the princes led there. Now, as we circled the amba with the ruins open to our gaze, I felt this mental picture crystallize.

'The roofs of the palace were turned into arches of mossy stone joined by a cement that grew harder with time, and the building stood from century to century deriding the solstitial rains and equinoctial hurricanes ... Here the sons of Abyssinia lived only to know the soft vicissitudes of pleasure ...' So runs Dr Johnson's description of the palace where Rasselas lived.

The princes on the Mountain in Dr Johnson's time certainly shared with Rasselas their melancholy situation – below them the Happy Valley sloped in terraces of green and gold to the edge of the surrounding hills – but they had little else in common. As the mossy walls on the cramped summit now reveal, the princes' abodes must have been ordinary stone-and-wattle huts. Regarding the 'soft vicissitudes of pleasure', there can have been little relief from the dour monotony of life on the Mountain except possibly in the ceremonies of the Church of Mariam, whose gabled walls are now overgrown. Here the princes must have spent much of their days praying either for resignation to their fate or for their hopes of succession to be realized. Bacuffa, for instance, vowed to found a Church of Mariam if he ever became King, and when in due course he succeeded to the throne he built a fine church at Webilla, close to Wehni. Besides the church the only other building of any importance on the Mountain was the Governor's palace (the 'great house' referred to by the old man who had climbed the

staircase). To the princes the Governor's palace must have borne a nostalgic air of Gondarin magnificence; rich brocades, silver-tipped spears and buffalo-hide shields inlaid with semi-precious stones, were all they had to recall the life they had left when they were sent to the Mountain.

The princes' life might thus appear both grim and drab – much like that of prisoners anywhere. But to the huts, the church and the Governor's palace, a fourth ingredient was added which gave life on the Mountain a melodramatic flavour; the staircase. Up its thousand steps came messengers carrying letters from the world outside, normally from the King to the Governor of the Mountain or from friends or family in Gondar. But once in a lifetime they would bring the electric news that the King had died and his successor chosen from one of the confined princes.

With what feelings would the fortunate prince then assume the delicate brocades of office and follow the pikemen and kettle-drummers down the staircase. Twenty

years he had waited and prayed for this day. And with what feelings would those remaining watch the cavalcade recede along the green paths of the Happy Valley, till lost to view behind the slopes of Cumbel and Tarara. Yesterday they had all been fellow sufferers in exile; now he was to be crowned King of Gondar, the anointed of God, and they were to be the objects of his clemency or the victims of his cruelty, as fate disposed. For a time the boom of the forty-five kettle-drummers that accompanied the King on the march would have echoed dully beyond Tarara, and then an ominous silence would have wrapped the Mountain like a cloud.

Three times the aeroplane circled the black stalactite of rock, dappled with kite's droppings and set in its cushion of green woods and pastures. Then with its shadow following obediently behind, the aeroplane flew off in a broad arc and the green valley faded into the blue haze behind us. The Mountain was still unravished; the mystical paradise of Mount Abora was not to be attained.

Epilogue

Je reviendrai avec des membres de fer, la peau sombre, l'oeuil furieux, sur mon masque on me jugera d'une race forte ... je serai oissif et brutal. Les femmes soignent ces feroces infirmes retour des pays chauds.

Rimbaud

When Rasselas escaped from the Happy Valley he descended to a port on the Red Sea, whence he took passage in a ship to Suez. For my part I flew to Aden, where I boarded a Union Castle steamer bound for England.

London seemed just as I had remembered it. Grey cliffs of apartment blocks, grey London grass, grey days in the office where the job that I had so long postponed had at last caught up with me.

The only difference in London that I could discern was that someone had coined a catch-phrase about 'The Establishment'; and people could not believe that I had never heard of a play called *Look Back in Anger*.

My friends seemed just as I had remembered them. They had heard from my sister that I had left Abyssinia, and made a full circuit of the globe. ('I got so bored with telling them you were still stuck in Abyssinia,' she told me later, 'that I said you'd gone to Nepal. From there you pushed on to Mongolia. I knew you'd expect it of me.') When my friends learnt the truth they hid their disappointment bravely.

Others less well known to me had heard even wilder reports. In the weeks succeeding my return I was asked if it was true that I had found princes still living on the Mountain fettered with chains of solid gold; that I had been captured by bandits and ransomed by the British Embassy; that I had married an Ethiopian princess in Aden; that I was going back to Addis as the press agent of the Lion of Judah. Somebody even asked me if I thought King Zog was secure on his throne. I began to try to forget about Ethiopia.

Yet one last act of piety to the Mountain remained unpaid.

Outside Paris, in the vault of the village church of Rueil is the grave of an Ethiopian called Zagachrist. This mysterious figure apparently left Ethiopia in 1632; two years later he arrived at the court of Louis XIV at Versailles. He claimed to be the rightful heir to the throne of Solomon, dispossessed by King Facilidas. If his claim was correct it would mean that he was one of the possible heirs to the throne who would, according to the practice lately revived by Facilidas, have been sent to the Mountain. If Zagachrist was not an impostor – which he may well have been – he must have been the only prince to escape from the Happy Valley to search for happiness, like Rasselas, in the hectic world beyond.

Zagachrist, it seems, enjoyed his brief span of freedom. His swarthy looks and his prowess as a lover intrigued the ladies of Versailles; he conducted a notorious affair with the wife of a deputy of the Parliament; several references to his amours are to be found in the letters of Mme de Sévigné. Eventually, for political reasons, he was taken up by Cardinal Richelieu and lodged at his château in Rueil. But Zagachrist's health was soon undermined by the dampness of the European climate and such unwonted high living. He died of bronchitis in 1638.

Once more I left England, and on a damp autumnal day I came to Rueil. A procession of plane trees led me towards the church; there was a smell of fresh bread and coffee in the streets; and the distant clatter of a suburban town.

Gravely I paid my respects to Zagachrist. Had he been sent to the Mountain? Had he stood on the summit of Wehni where I shall never stand – looking out on the flowers and rills of the Happy Valley below? My quest, at any rate, was ended. With a sombre feeling of finality I read the epitaph to Zagachrist:

Ci gist, le roi d'Ethiopie,
L'original ou la copie.
Le fut-il? ne le fut-il pas?
La mort a fini les debats.

(Here lies the king of Ethiopia,
The original or a copy?
Was he? Or was he not?
Death ends the debate.)

Postscript

For the next forty-two years I dreamt romantic dreams of landing on the Mountain by helicopter.

Enter Dan Spencer, pilot of Bell helicopter Papa X-Ray Charlie, and the answer to any explorer's prayer. Dan is a daredevil 32-year-old engineer–pilot from Upper State New York, whose passion is to fly helicopters for the Baptist mission in Ethiopia. He has flashing blue eyes, gold epaulettes and a silver-and-scarlet machine inscribed 'Helimission'. Most of the time he flies rescue missions, like Dan Dare, the hero of the comic strip, saving people from famine and flood.

On the telephone Dan had seemed very confident. 'I've yet to see an Ethiopian amba where I can't land my helicopter.' But I showed him my photographs of that 1,000-high rocky thumb, taken through the cabin window of the Dakota forty-two years before. Dan warned me we might be in trouble. 'You see, if it's too hairy to land, you won't be able to jump. The insurance makes it a no-no.'

As the turbo-prop howled and whined on the runway, Dan prayed aloud to the Lord to give his blessing to our trip. And then we were off, and up and over Addis Ababa, heading north–west across the smooth green tableland.

Two hours later we were circling Amba Wehni, taking our place in a spiral of hundreds of brown kites and black vultures. 'Boy,' the pilot of the Dakota had said all those years ago, 'what a goddam place to spend your life – among the birds.' The amba was white with bird lime, like a cliff projecting from the sea. Dan said nothing. He was staring hard at a small patch of brown grass between two candelabra cacti. It was the nearest thing to a flat piece of ground. My earphones crackled. 'We'll do another circuit ... The air's very thin at this altitude ... downdrafts of 1,000 feet a minute...'

Then Dan came to a decision. If we tried to land we'd be splashed all over the Mountain. And if I tried to jump there'd be no way back. So the best I could do was to explore the summit with a telephoto lens.

The summit is about 80 yards by 40 yards square, the size of two tennis-courts. The only building of any size is the church which I could see more clearly than before, now in ruins, with a barrel vault and a gabled roof build in limestone and pink tufa in the Gondarin style. I suppose the ceiling may have been once decorated with angels – like the roof of the famous church of Debra Berhan at Gondar. Here the wretched princes must have had some relief from this gulag in the sky. But food and water would always have been short because there was no spring on the summit and no room to grow grain or vegetables. Everything had to be brought up those 1,000 steps from below.

I noticed one other astonishing feature of Wehni. I had always imagined the royal prisoners would have enjoyed a magnificent view over the surrounding valley, like the princes in the Happy Valley of Johnson's Rasselas. In fact the ruins of a wall surround the entire summit, as the wall surrounds the palaces of Gondar. The prisoners at Wehni would have had nothing to see but the birds.

•

After half a dozen circuits we landed on the grassy terrace beside the mountain. Before the engines had stopped, several hundred villagers were sweeping down towards us. Dan sounded the hooter to keep them away from the rotors. They were wild-looking men dressed in shammas and barefooted like their children. It was clear that, poor as they were, their population had trebled in the last forty years. Materially, little had changed, apart from the new huts sprawling down the green slopes. But there was a new spirit at Wehni which I could not miss. Gone was the scrupulous politeness towards strangers. The grandchildren of the villagers, who had bowed low to me forty years before, now pushed and jostled like a football crowd.

Yet we found one old patriarch who remembered my previous visit. 'But you were younger then.' I showed him the book I had written and the photograph of the Mountain taken from the Dakota. What did he think of the fate of the princes up there with the birds? 'It was all right at the beginning, when there were few of them, the first generation of princes. There was plenty of food for them. Later, when there were hundreds up there, there were difficulties ...' I wondered if his great grandfather had been one of the jailers who had to climb the 1,000 steps morning and evening.

Dan was sounding the hooter, anxious to be off before somebody got struck by the rotors. It was time to go. Wehni had lost its innocence.

Index

PICTURE CREDITS

Line drawings on pp. 1, 34–5, 51, 64–5, 69, 75, 84–5, 112–113, 127, 130–31, 147, 160 are by Susan Benson (née Campbell) from original drawings in the 1959 edition of this book; the lithographs reproduced on pp 2–3, 4–5, 16, 80–81, 90–91, 124–5, 150–51, 164–5, 165, 166–7 are from Scenes in Ethiopia, 1852, by John Martin Bernatz, Artist to the British Mission to the Court of Shoa (on the Harris Mission to Ethiopia, 1841–3), photographed by Martin Norris; the background map on pp. 4-5, 6-7, 19, 28, 43, 55, 69, 101, 128, 140–41, and the lithograph on pp. 69 are taken from The Prester John of the Indies, by Fr. Francisco Alvarez, priest, revised and edited by C. F. Bekingham and G. W. B. Huntingford (Cambridge UP, 1961); maps on pp. 7, 43, 101, 128, 151 are painted by Stephen Conlin, based on sketch maps in the 1959 edition; the drawings on p. 9 (back), and on pp. 26–7, 30, 36–7, 38–9, 43, 58–9, 80, 101, 128, 134, are from Travels to Discover the Source of the Nile (1790), by James Bruce of Kinnaird, photographed by Martin Norris: the map on p. 9 (front) is Aethiopia (Abyssinia), by Johan Blaeu c. 1635, reproduced by permission of the Royal Geographical Society; the lithograph on p. 20 comes from George Viscount Valentia's Voyages and Travels (London, 1809: 3 vols); the photograph on pp. 146–7 was taken by Antonia Pinter, and that on p. 173 was taken by Richard Illingworth; the illustration on p. 155 is from an eighteenth-century manuscript in the British Museum; and the 1720 edition of Milton's Paradise Lost on p. 176 was photographed by Visualeyes. All other photographs were taken by the author.

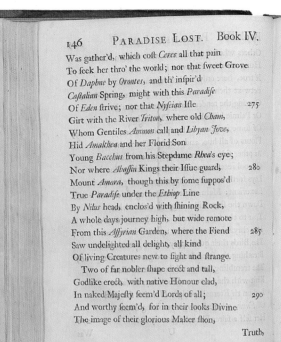

First published in the United Kingdom in 1959,
this edition in 1998 by Weidenfeld & Nicolson

This paperback edition first published in 1999 by
Seven Dials, Illustrated Division,
The Orion Publishing Group
Wellington House, 125 Strand
London, WC2R 0BB

Distributed in the United States of America by
Sterling Publishing Co., Inc.
387 Park Avenue South,
New York, NY 10016-8810
A CIP catalogue record for this book is available
from the British Library

ISBN 1 84188 005 1

Photography: Thomas Pakenham
Edited by Penny Gardiner
Photographs of Bruce and Bernatz plates: Martin Norris
Map artist: Stephen Conlin
Cartography: Advanced Illustration
Printed and bound in Italy
Set in: Garamond